MATHEMATICS OF FAILURES

AKSHAY PARIJA

BLACK EAGLE BOOKS

USA address:
7464 Wisdom Lane
Dublin, OH 43016

India address:
E/312, Trident Galaxy, Kalinga Nagar,
Bhubaneswar-751003, Odisha, India

E-mail: info@blackeaglebooks.org
Website: www.blackeaglebooks.org

Second International Edition Published by
BLACK EAGLE BOOKS, 2025

MATHEMATICS OF FAILURES
Akshay Parija

Copyright © **Akshay Parija**

All rights reserved. No part of this publication may be reproduced, stored in a retrieval system, or transmitted, in any form or by any means, electronic, mechanical, photocopying, recording or otherwise without the prior permission of the publisher.

ISBN- 978-1-64560-661-1 (Paperback)

Printed in the United States of America

To Err is human, to forgive is divine!!!

Alexander Pope

Dedicated to all who understood me and remained with me thru good and bad times..

The book is neither a work of linguistic or literary excellence.

Extremely grateful to :

Payal Parija
Vikram Gowda
Shiv Parija Gowda
&
Shree K Rajeev Kumar
For the big task of editing and correction.

Contents

1. MATHEMATICS OF FAILURES,
   The Prelude: 7
2. Mathematics of Failures
   THE REFLECTIONS (APRIL 2022) 10
3. THE STRANGE CONFLUENCE:
   ART AND MONEY 14
4. THUKUL :
   THE CULTURAL JOURNEY 35
5. THE KADVISACH OF KADVIHAWA 50
6. BIG DREAM WENT SOWER!! 60
7. TRUST AND DESTINY 71
8. THE WET HEAVENS 91
9. THE NEW CHALLENGE
   OF COPY FILM 100
10. THE MAKING OF PAIKA BIDROH 107
11. THE BENGAL JOURNEY:
    TO THE LAND OF CREATIVITY 114
12. DREAMS, UNCERTAINTY AND
    UNKNOWN JOURNEY 142
13. THE BUSINESS INFINITY 164
14. A LIFE TRANSFORMED 173
15. THE JOURNEY TO DESTRUCTION 180
16. AMID THE CATASTROPHE 198

THE BANKER

THE FILM MAKER

MATHEMATICS OF FAILURES, The Prelude:

In my poetic understanding of 'Arithmetic,' it relates to figures only. Whereas "mathematics" include arithmetic that deal in numbers, trigonometry that analyses from both sides and geometry, that analyses various angles.

In arithmetic, wrong calculation or figures end in total mistakes, fetching zero value. Whereas in comprehensive mathematics, we do not end up in zero value for our actions. You may still fetch few numbers if the steps were taken correctly.

In life, a mistake may end you up in a problem, but during later part of the life, it may turn out to be positive.

Here, I am not ashamed to share the mathematics of my life. I have gone wrong in many decisions of my life and suffered, but the decisions were not always wrong. It was not taken based on pure arithmetic of personal benefit or material gains.

There is no decision taken in life or our daily routine which can be said right or wrong.

When I went to study the Executive MBA (ADVANCE MANAGEMENT PROGRAMME) at Harvard Business School, USA, (HBS), and before joining the programme, I got a large packet of study material that I should read well before the first class at HB. Of course, in later days' study materials got digitalized to an IPAD. It was a lot of material of do's and donot's besides many case studies which was the basis of studies in the management education popularly known as "case study method".

Having left regular studies long back after getting into the professional life, it was scary for me to be able to study those voluminous study material in detail. Nevertheless, I put my best efforts, may be due to the realization that a significant course fee has been paid.

The first basic learning I got was that there is no decision which is right or wrong. A decision taken at a particular time after genuine due diligence could be at best right at that point of time. Later on, it could be reverse; a right decision could go wrong and a wrong decision probably could have been right. It was the best at that circumstance. Life dynamics change and circumstances change. So also decisions that was best today could go wrong during later days or vice versa.

Many a times we refer to some people as "men with golden touch". Whatever he/she touches turns into gold and some people are always right in their decisions. Some get it wrong. Brave do not repent on their decision if it goes wrong many times. They work towards correcting it and make it right to carry on with the next.

Tenzing Norgey and Edmund Hilary would have never climbed Mount Everest if they would not have taken the mathematical decision to continue to climb or for that matter Neil Armstrong landing on moon. If they would have done arithmetical calculations of many probabilities of failures, they would not have achieved what they achieved today.

Mrs Sonia Gandhi unfortunately failed to be Prime Minister of India though her arithmetic was with her but Dr Manmohan Singh ruled for 10 years. Someone's arithmetic was right, but mathematics was wrong.

It is not my intention to show anybody wrong nor hurt the decision of anybody, but only reflect on my both arithmetical or mathematical calculations.

In this book of reflections of my life, I endeavor to highlight that I did go wrong many times in life but some were arithmetical failures but mathematical success for which I am where I am today Living a wonderful life in the shadows of love, regrets, success, failures and more.

● ● ●

Mathematics of Failures

THE REFLECTIONS (APRIL 2022)

Sitting on seat 1A on an Indigo flight to Bangkok from Kolkata airport was a significant qualitative transformation for me from the seat of 1A in Emirates.

In those days it used to be Dubai to Bangkok in the Sky Cabin of Airbus 380. Normally the first class in Emirates is the upper deck of the newly introduced Airbus 380. Being a frequent business traveler and a platinum member, Emirates used to extend special invites during the introduction of the Airbus A380 routes to various destinations advising me to adjust my travel dates and experience the new generation massive aircraft Airbus A380. On arrival, we used to be treated special with a certificate of being the first flier with mementos to remember.

Today as I travel with the budget airline Indigo getting the 1A seat with slightly larger legroom by paying about Rs.2500/- more, I was remembering the contrast after one and half decades of flying on Emirates, three decades of international flying and post COVID days of restrictions and recessions.

Unlike the 1A of Emirates with a large TV screen, full bed convertible seat, welcome champagne with costly assorted nuts, one has to be lucky in Indigo to elbow out the ever-pushing passengers who, rush to the plane as if the aircraft will go away without them.

Somehow after being seated in 1A with a lot of difficulties to place my small computer bag overhead, I settled on my seat. Many times, fliers will place their larger than normal hand bags in the first-row overhead and coolly go to their back of the aircraft seats leaving no room for the front row travelers to place their handbags. Somehow the budget airlines till date have never shown sympathy or alternates for this inconvenience. Probably a simple announcement that one should place their hand bag close to his or her seat will bring the change.

Being a regular traveller, I had pre-booked a vegetarian sandwich, two Black Level scotches and a tiny tin of salted cashew nuts. It was extremely inconvenient in the small seats of budget airlines to place all these things in a mini tray. Since the route was bumpy I could not takeout my notebook to use the time to write or catch up on some films or entertainment.

In Emirates first class sky cabin, as soon we take off and seat belt signs are off, the ever energetic and of course beautiful hostess come with a menu of exotic drinks like vintage scotches, single malt whiskeys and best of the collections of wines and spirits. Due to their excellent customer relationship management software, they would even know my preference and the first approach would be "Mr. Parija, would you prefer your normal vodka martini today or you wish to try our best of other selections". The drinks come in the tray with my preferred savory of caviar, assorted Arabic mezze or steamed prawns. Food will be served only when I am ready to eat. Drinks will be repeated till one wishes. In a flight of 8 hours costing about Rs.3.5lacs return fare, few drinks of world-class brands, the great selection of food served only when you order and the grand ambiance makes up over the Rs. 24,000 costing the budget airlines travel. The value for money, ambience, convenience, and the great comfort makes it significantly appropriate to fly Emirates.

Emirates extends a complementary fast track card, so we jump the long queues at immigration where in one can be stuck for hours in a serpentine queue.

The arithmetic of travel in budget airlines may be right due to the low fare but the mathematics was not right for the experience of travel. Moreover, at some stage in life we go for arithmetic than mathematics with ups and downs in our life journey.

● ● ●

THE STRANGE CONFLUENCE: ART AND MONEY

If I would travel back in time, I could go back to December 2001, almost 24 years back. At the age of 44 and so called success in career as well as financial stability, there was nothing that could offer me the motivation to look forward to in my banking carrier. I had reached a significant C-suite position. Back at that time, probably no other person from Odisha had reached this position in the Middle East Banking scene. However today significant number of Odiyas are in top positions making all of us proud for their global achievements.

Drawing a big cost to company (CTC) package, it was enough satisfaction that I cannot aspire for more.

In our management debates in the bank I worked, talent snatching by competitors was always matter of concerns and discussions. My normal argument used to be put a high value on the talent so that it will be difficult for the employee to switch job as competitors cannot afford to pay so much. Alternatively, the employee will also have limited options to switch jobs.

I was paid high not to be retained but being in business banking that included corporate and wholesale business, earning contribution to the organization is easily measurable and obviously my contribution was always significantly high.

My popularity as a dynamic banker in Sultanate of Oman was due to my quick decision making skills, service focus and known as a provider of comprehensive business solutions. The positive reputation did not remain limited to Oman, but also reached my home state of Odisha.

During one of my normal visits to Odisha in the month of December 2001, I was warmly invited by a common friend to a party at the poolside of an upcoming star hotel in Bhubaneswar. Initially a bit hesitant being an outsider, I was persuaded to be there. On arrival, most interestingly I found myself to be at home as I found I almost knew everyone either as close acquaintances or people I had met on somewhere in some social occasion.

The main host or the owner of the upcoming hotel was a dynamic business group led by two equally dynamic businessmen Mr. Rohit Das and Mr. Pramod Rath.

Extremely humble, friendly, and articulate, both welcomed me with unusual warmth. First time in Bhubaneswar I witnessed a poolside party with a congregation of professionals, doctors, engineers, bureaucrats, and businessmen.

The party was quite at par with any of our overseas big parties in star hotels. Excellent drinks of best international brands were flowing liberally in spite of import restrictions those days. Food spread was unthinkable with great choices and varieties. The best of prawns, crabs, fish in many varieties were there. Anything you opt for in veg or nonveg was there.

There were two surprise guests who did not drink but were the star of the evening. They were in high spirit without any spirit.

The first among the rare two was the highly successful Er Tushar Mishra. Though I was not very acquainted with him, I had heard a lot about him everywhere in Bhubaneswar. Mr Mishra with four of his friends from NIT Rourkela had decided not to take up coveted Government jobs which would have fallen in their laps being first class students. Instead, they chose to be entrepreneurs in 1980. Warmly encouraged by the dynamic leader of Odisha Shri Basant Biswal who always encouraged local people of Odisha, they brought in a renaissance in contracting activity by infusing modern technology into the traditional contracting of Odisha. B Engineers, as the name of the company. B Engineers was not a traditional 'Contracting Company' but transformed to a much respected 'Engineering and Construction Company'. They were probably the first Construction Group with acumen, expertise and infrastructure to take up Civil, Electrical, Mechanical and much advanced, complicated Railway bridges or Barrages.

Having gone thru both glory and downfalls as happens in business with political changes, they were back to strong reckoning in Odisha. They were obviously compared to engineering giants like Larsen & Tubro or Hindustan Constructions in Odisha.

Their visible achievements which was talk of the town was the long demanded Cuttack Railway Overbridge that they could complete in 18 months against the scheduled 24 months. Unlike most of the contractors who are perennially late in completing their work, they were able to achieve timely delivery thru design, planning and professional execution.

Mr Tushar Mishra as Chairman and MD lead from the front to take the company to a much higher level. Be it the overbridges, or Indoor Stadium or Mahanadi Barrage or the first Public Private Partnership(PPP) multi storied Housing Projects, they were visible everywhere. They were the first to introduce multi use steal scaffolding in Odisha compared to the earlier bamboo and wood scaffolding.

I had a warm introduction with Mr Mishra by the hosts. As he was a tee totter, our communication in the party was brief though it created a strong foundation of association in later part of life.

The other guest was the star at the function, Minister of Higher Education and Rural Development. Ever young and heartthrob of Odiya Cinema, Mr Prasant Nanda, the actor, the director, the writer, the composer, the screenplay writer all in one.

It can be said God had done injustice having loaded all talents in one person. A first time election contestant, winner with significant margin and selected in an important ministry allotted to a first time MLA under Shri Naveen Patnaik, the new Chief Minister, who later on, created the biggest history in Odisha politics.

Rightly or wrongly known to be a well-known Odiya in the Middle East, more so due to my help in creating employment for many Odiya's in the tax free haven of Middle East, I was warmly introduced to Mr Prasant Nanda by my hosts.

I was thunder stuck with man and the actor. I was his biggest fan, in whose cinematic journey of late seventies, I had grown up in my school and college studies and whose name is a house hold name in Odisha was standing in front of me. Ideally, I would have waited hours to have a glimpse of him around his shooting sets but today; I am being introduced in a friendly atmosphere not as a fan but with the respect of being a well-known NRI.

Mr Prasant Nanda was indeed a charmer. He was exceptionally courteous, nice and warm. In a moment he bought my loyalty with a humane line "we must meet in your land abroad. I have heard of the spectacular landscape of Sultanate of Oman". His simplicity won me over and I had a very positive feeling next few days having met a star of Odisha, that too who has grown to be a successful politician. What midas touch this man has that whatever he ventures into, has turned gold.

Life went on. Bhubaneswar's most popular and fabulous hotel of that time "The Crown" got inaugurated. Slowly getting close to the promoters and moreover finding them to be excellent entrepreneurs, I developed a close fondness for the owners group. Foremost was the Chairman of the hotel Shri Rohit Das. We instantly developed an unlimited undefined and unselfish bonding. Mr Das forced me to stay in the hotel whenever I visited Bhubaneswar. Over the period Crown became my home address in Bhubaneswar for next 18 years.

However, going back in time to those days, Mr. Rohit Das, the Chairman of the hotel grew to be like a younger brother to me from being a friend and we bonded significantly sharing many personal agonies and ecstasy.

The night I had my late mother's 11th Day function at Hotel Crown to the anxiety of my siblings of holding the same in a Star Hotel instead of a temple premises after her journey heavenly abode, I told Mr. Rohit Das, that what is left in my body should also travel from his hotel. He got so upset, he shouted at me for the first and last time. Luck and life is so strange, a decade later I had to see his final journey from the hotel. His son owes me his father's wish that he will also give mukhagni to me on my last journey. My only daughter's marriage also took place in the hotel and it remained for a long period to be one of the best reception in the town.

Obviously, I was honest in my emotional expression of my death rituals and Mr Das was spontaneous with his affectionate reaction.

Mr Das, unfortunately thru a misconceived conspiracy got into a legal problem during 2006/07 and his business sadly suffered great losses. A warm, friendly and genuine person as he was, everybody came forward to help him and he again did rise like a phoenix to his past glory.

During few years in early 2000, I had become a significant promoter of Odishi Dance all across the globe.

In October 2007, Mr Das called me and informed me that Mr Prasant Nanda had planned to make a film, not in his usual box office formula but something very different. He wishes to experiment with "world cinema". Mr Das had assured Mr Nanda to support for the film but due to his unfortunate legal complications, he was unable to do so. I must admit that I had no intention or ambitions to make films. However, since Mr Das requested to meet such a big man I proposed Mr. Nanda visit Muscat, Oman, spend a few days with me and we can surely discuss the story and take it forward to a logical end.I arranged a visa in one day, sent a first class flight ticket to Mr Nanda who was not coming to solicit finance but for me a superstar, a legend, the *Bheesma Peetamaha* of Odia cinema is visiting my home. This was his first visit abroad. At the airport I arranged a VVIP reception for him to avoid the tension of immigration. The special welcome was very immaterial for him as he had seen it all in his life as a superstar as well as a senior Cabinet Minister.

That evening, I unfortunately had an official engagement. We sat down to talk at 9 pm on my return from the engagement at the private lounge upstirs next to my bedroom.

My usual day starts at 5am every morning. I hit the gym at 5.30am at Grand Hyatt Club, back home at 6.45 am, get ready and get into the car at 7am. The houseboy packs me a sandwich made of egg white omelet with two brown bread slices wrapped in an aluminum foil. I savor my breakfast on the way in the car as I drive to office 15 minutes away while enjoying some great music with the high standard acoustics in the luxury car that I drive. The day ends by about 8.30pm due to the voluminous work responsibilities of a senior banker.

By 9 pm I am home and after a shower I sit in front of TV in the lounge for the day's news. The rare single malts on the TV room table and fish fry of Rohu/Ilsha available of high quality from Bangladesh as accompaniment was my life routine and my luxury to look forward to most of the evenings when I am home, not invited to any official or private parties.

As I joined Mr. Nanda in the TV room with the single malt, his face was visibly uncomfortable. He does not drink and probably wished to talk very formally without drinks.

It did not take me long to convince him of my lifestyle of hard work in the day and relaxation in the evenings. In any case he did not have a choice than to tolerate me. But my humble behavior and narration of my life of hard work and looking forward to relaxation with few drinks and Odia style fish fry probably made him comfortable. Later part in life or next decade of relationship, he would rather arrange the best collection of fish preparations for me at Bhubaneswar whenever I visit, knowing my love for it.

Sharing the couch with Mr Prasant Nanda was in itself a great honor and I had to keep pinching myself that its true, not a dream.

We spoke and continued the conversation till mid night. A habitual drinker of many pegs, I was mesmerized after my first drink to listen to him and I forgot about the refill.

My house boy cum barman was surprised, but never intervened the refill.

By midnight for "The Living Ghost", (Jiaanta Bhoota) was perceived, conceived and awaited to take birth.

xxxxxxxxxxxxxxx

In 1974, after the graduation classes got over in December, we students start preparations for the final examination normally held around the month of March. As I was joining my closest friend Mr Bikram Singh Deo fondly nicknamed Bugee, at his house for the joint preparation for the exams, I volunteered to assist his sister for two hours in morning from 7 am to 9am, who was running a newly started nursery school. She was magnanimously paying me Rs 100 for my work which was a significantly high amount in 1974.

At the Nursery, Parents of toddlers of four to six years found me an interesting person to talk. One of the parents, Mr G.K.Panda who used to work in a Bank, voluntarily from his side one day, asked me why I do not think of joining the bank service as a cashier/clerk. He emphasized that the salary is reasonable, and I could always pursue my higher education as well as ambitions of life after my college and university education.

Mr Panda was a Trade Union Leader of the Non Officer Union of the bank and was always willing to help Non Officer cadre employees of the bank. I found him to be genuine, spontaneous and humble.

Thus, an Economics and Political Science student with ambitions of cracking civil services or to be a businessman ended up getting selected as shroff/store keeper (a very typical old designation for Cashier cum Store Keeper) with Indian Overseas Bank in March 1975. Mr Panda advised me that I should not hesitate to consent for a posting in the then undivided Koraput District by personally assuring me to help in getting me a transfer back to Cuttack or Bhubaneswar soon.

In early 1975, I joined the bank for training at Rayagada, then under undivided Koraput district. I was groomed to join a new branch opening at Bissam Cuttack, closer to a mountain range called Niyamgiri. Rayagada was a small town with two small cinema halls but hardly any decent restaurants to eat. The town had visible Telugu speaker's presence. The training period was interesting learning about banking.

Seven days into Bissam Cuttack with opening of the new branch comes the Rathayatra that gets celebrated in many places in Odisha and across India.

Bissam Cuttack in 1975 was a very small village. It had a morum (red pebbles)road, running one end where a mission hospital was operational to other end of the place where there were small government offices

offices like, block office, Tahasil office, a U.P School and a small government hospital. Doctors rarely are there and the hospital was practically run by the compounder who is as much respected and was called 'Doctor Babu'.

A passenger bus used to pass through Bissam Cuttack in morning coming from Rayagada going to Muniguda that returns in the evening.

A lady in her early forties and probably a widow, used to have a small thatched housed eating place where one can have a meal with only 75 paisa. While she was still looking desirable, her daughter in her spring years with good looks and a youthful body was special attraction for young people. She used to serve while her mother cooked the food. She would be clad in a cotton saree and an ill-fitting blouse that would unintentionally reveal her bust line. She would sportingly accept various humorous comments of appreciation from the visitors. The thali contained rice, dal, few local vegetables curry and with 25 paisa more, a small piece of local fish curry was served. If one orders in advance, for one rupee one could get mutton curry. In other places around block office, there used to be shops selling grocery, kerosene etc. Though there was electricity connection in Bissam Cuttack, few houses had taken electricity connection. There was one street bulb near mission hospital and another near block office. Otherwise, the streets were dark.

On the day of Rathyatra, a small handmade wooden chariot was pulled for about 500 meters, but the gathering in those days used to be in large numbers. Many small toy shops, eateries, fancy item shops sprang up along the road and their petromax lights used to illuminate the darkness. In rural language it was a "Mela".

That day, after banking hours at 5pm, I also walked down to the festival site, hardly hundred meters away.

I was 19 years old, fresh from college and very new to interiors of Odisha, being born and brought up in coastal Odisha of Cuttack/Bhubaneswar. What stuck my attention was few groups of people, men, women, young girls and boys holding hands and moving together as a group.

I did not see any fear of worry in their faces but a strange look of pure simplicity. I could not see in their body language any consciousness for their body language for the scant clothes they were wearing. Women, young or old, were hardly able to cover their bust line with clothes, but it definitely was covered with flowers and some typical rural jewelry.

Looking at my interest for them, I was warned by a local acquaintance to be careful, not to go near them which may be irritating to them. The men in groups were holding an axe like weapon which is supposed to be part of their costume, but they all looked very relaxed and in a happy mood. It appeared everything was fanciful for them. I was told they are Dongria Kandha community and live 7km a top mountain Niyamgiri. Their life revolved around sunlight and at best wooden fire in nights They come down to the plains only twice in a year to sell their agriculture produce after harvest or during Rathyatra festival.

Though my optional subject was Psychology in college, but Anthropology was my hobby. Getting quite inquisitive about the community, next Sunday accompanied by three other local people, we trekked 7KM on the hills and reached the peak mountain area with very sparse inhabition of Dongria Community in small handmade jhopdis, that barely can save you from heavy rain. Handmade thatched one room house with clear courtyards, cooking is done outside and each household will have their loyal pets such as goats, cows, chicken etc roaming freely.

We had planned to stay the night as by the time we reached it was about 4PM and almost getting dark.

As I went thru an acquaintance of the community, we were fed a dinner of an item which was like a khichdi made of Rice, and a typical local lentil called

Kandula and cooked with great affection. It genuinely tested great. As we were all youngsters, we were invited to their evening entertainment of Dhangda/Dhangdi place.

Young girls and boys assemble there in evening after the full day of hard work. They drink a locally brewed wine. They sing and dance to their heartfull.

Significantly after few hours of entertainment, men sleep in a dormitory and women sleep in another dormitory. No sexual advances or sex until marriage. A great moral learning!! And how happiness is just a feeling. The dormitory is no luxury, but scantily covered thatched sheds with grounds well leveled. All sleep on the floor.

The entire community had one binding force "The Niyamgiri Raja". King of Niyamgiri mountain. The lover courts his beloved and promises that after marriage he will take her to Niyamgiri Raja. On death it is said that the dead have gone to Niyamgiri Raja. And on a child birth it is said that the child was given by Niyamgiri Raja.

Such strong simplistic faith !! And, all believe the Niyamgiri Raja is extremely rich.!!

Thirty-Two years later when I was listening to the story narration from Sri Prashant Nanda, without words and without intruptions. I did not require my single malt refill. I was saying to myself that what I witnessed 32 years back was true and today Niyamgiri mountain is estimated to have Six Billion Dollar worth of Bauxite Deposit.

The mountain will be blasted to ground. All the inhabitants of the Dongaria Kandha community will be homeless.

Mr. Nanda was unfortunately a bit out of political limelight at that time and his creativity and energy level wanted to do more. He was restless day and night. This restlessness at home was conveyed to me by his son counselling me to help him do the film. His son reassured me that if I don't get my money back, he has a large land near Chandaka and he will part with a part of the land to at least recover my investments. It surely reflected an assurance of Mr. Nanda's commitment for the film.

The innocent habitants of Niyamgiri will be homeless, jobless and will be on the street. Saddest is their heaven of an innocent non-corrupt living will be lost forever.

And here I am to take a decision, Arithmetic or Mathematics, to produce the film as a business or as a passion to bring the plight of a community to limelight.

It was not an arithmetic decision to make. Irrespective of few other friends objecting to it, I was disturbed from inside about the plight of the people that I so closely observed thirty-two years back.

Mr Prashant Nanda gave an estimate of Rs 61 lacs budget with the best Director of Photography and most revered Sri Apurba Kishore Bir to work on it and Sri Anup Chatterjee to do sound design. Both had multiple National Awards to their Credit.

Money paid and I become a hesitant film producer in life for the first time which I never aimed for, desired for or dreamed fo.

The film The Living Ghost (Jiaanta Bhoota) carefully reflected the innocence of the Dongria Kandha community, their blind faith in God and their exploitation by people down in valleys with education and knowledge. The film reflected a girl sexually exploited is not guilty but the people doing exploitation are feeling guilty. The film depicted a woman can do any sacrifice for her man.

Mr Prashant Nanda used all his experience and expertise of life time to make this film. He selected the best of artists from Film and Theaters and the film came out as a wonder.

The film went to six International film festivals, got awards and recognition at Cairo, Egypt, Seattle, USA, Muscat Oman and few other countries. International Festivals were not as many as today nor the selections were that easy. Besides, I was not so experienced on the processes of sending films to international festivals. The selected few had stringent quality specifications and it used to be an honor to just get selected, forget awarded. Contrary to today with mushrooming festivals in all corners of world, a selection, genuine or manipulated, makes headlines in social media and news hungry local print media.

Over the making of film at Rs.61 lacs, the cost of showcasing it all around the World probably costed me over Rs.40 lacs including travels and stays at festivals abroad.

The film won National Award for Best Film on Environment Protection, probably the only film till that time from Odisha to win an Award under National

(National Award from President of India for the Best Film on Conservation of Environment)

Award category unlike the best regional films category which many had won from Odisha.

The film went on to win a record breaking 7 State Film Awards as Best Film, Best Director, Best Cinematography, Best Editing, Best Jury award for the Heroine and Best Art Direction.

As fondly quoted by the Editor of the oldest Odiya Film Magazine in Odisha, Chalachitra Jagat, the film harvested awards around the world throughout the year 20_ _.

The film had no takers, lot of awards and recognition, but no buyer or viewers. I was not conversant on the art of distribution nor social media was that savvy those days to reach a larger audience.

Finally, it was sold to Tarang TV for Rs.6 lacs against a total cost of one crore rupees and that was the final income from the film.

No one ever bothered to ask the financial fate of the film other than Sri Rohit Das. He always regretted me in private that why he introduced me to a project where I would lose money. He was very happy to be invited to the prestigious National Award function at Bigyan Bhawan of New Delhi but still cribbed on the fact that the film did not recover cost, forget make any profit.

All assurances of recovering money return were forgotten. Promises were forgotten and I ended with an all almost Rs94 lacs loss in those days' worth few crores if sensitized to inflation index today.

The arithmetic was terribly wrong.

But mathematics?? National Awards, International Awards, State Awards!!

And the creation of awareness of Niyamgiri in the world! "Dongaria Kandh" became known for their life and miseries.

Reportedly a BBC reporter saw the film in an International Film Festival and reported extensively in news on the demise or extinguishing of a community who have tremendous multi decade old faith on the mountain as God. Consequently, the Church of England withdrew its investments with the mining company. A cascading effect started with multiple demonstrations and legal cases.

Eventually the mining lease of Niyamgiri was cancelled. I was invited to attend a large public event after the cancellation of the mining lease. I politely declined as my intention was to bring the plightly agony of a community, so simple and helpless. Not to get glory out of the circumstances.

I don't know what really happened in that Pure Land of Niyamgiri today.

But I think my mathematics of taking on the first venture of making the film was right!!

● ● ●

THUKUL :
THE CULTURAL JOURNEY

My eleven years of schooling till Matriculation was spent at Jagannathpur High School, Uradh Kiranti Senior Basic School and MS Academy. The Senior Basic School was an Ashram Model School where besides education, other curricular activities like Agriculture, Weaving, Drama etc were also a part of educational curriculum.

None of the schools had either electricity, sanitation or proper class rooms. We studied sitting down on the floor. During my last two years at Jaganathpur

High School, there was proper class room set up, with wooden chair and table for each student.

Unlike today, we at home in the mornings before going to school and no midday meals. We used to eat pronounce nights' leftover rice and go to school. Next food was after returning home and eat the leftover food cooked at lunch time. Playing hours used to be after the school hours during late afternoons. The agony of empty stomach was never a botheration against the excitement of playing.

The area was very underdeveloped. No electricity or water or proper sanitation. For all villagers, day starts with sun rising and ends up with sunset. Very few houses had kerosene lanterns. Moonlit nights were a luxury. During the fifteen days of lunar month, it was dark nights. Coming out of home even for urination was a matter of great fear of ghosts and witches which was supposed to be roaming around freely in the night.

With zero exposure to the outside world, no radio or newspaper, studies were the only activity we had to do other than rare opportunity to play of a milder form of kabaddi or football with very poor-quality balls.

I got addicted to reading cheap content novels published in Kolkata for the poorly educated labor class from Odisha working in various mills, mostly jute mills or cloth mills (chatakala or jhotakala). Those books were mostly sexually titillating to cater to the thousands of laborers living single lives. Later on by Class Seven onwards I got introduced to powerful literature from highly reputed authors of Odiya including Sri Bibhuti Patnaik who remained the most favorite for his well-crafted love stories with depiction of great social divide.

College life was again studies, struggle for existence and strenuous journey towards making a career.

Life flew fast from 1975 when I took up my first job as a cashier in Indian Overseas Bank till 2002 a Senior Banker job at Bank Muscat. I had got a coveted job with an International Bank at Kuwait in 1983 and had moved to Muscat, Oman by 1991 after the Kuwait War. I had established myself as a senior corporate banker with my single-minded devotion to be successful in life. The Harvard educated CEO, who had identified my sincerity and hard work had extended all support and encouragement. A great team of seniors, peers and juniors, we were a formidable team of aggressive bankers, and we together converted a bankrupt bank to the number one bank in 6 years. The reward was a rare recognition and came with great offers and opportunities. My career jumped multi fold and I became inspiration of many.

It was during this period I was requested to meet a top-level bureaucrat who happened to be the elder brother of a close friend for decades. I was requested by the revered gentleman to arrange an Odissi Dance show in Muscat for his daughter who was emerging as a renowned dancer. He encouraged me that the Ambassador to Oman will extend all help for the show.

My first question to myself was what is Odissi Dance? I had no knowledge of the art and culture of Odisha. I had to ask an acquaintance about Odissi Dance. Google was not active or operational in those days in my part of the world.

After listening about the attributes of the proud Odiya dance form Odissi, I had no hesitation to put all my efforts and resources into arranging the performance.

On a trip to Bhubaneswar few days later I enquired again with few friends and acquaintances about Odissi Dance as I was still ignorant on the exact type of performance. There were no YouTube or DVD/VCDs to see a performance.

I got a shock of my life for which I am ashamed till date. Few acquaintances made very lewd and obscene comments of the loose character of dancers, casting aspersions on me on my newfound interest for Odissi so that beautiful girls will be available for sexual pleasures. Supposedly aspiring dancers will do any sexual compromise for their career.

It had a devastating effect on me and I could not sleep next few days. A novice in dance knowledge, I had acquired some knowledge by that time about the grandeur and greatness of the dance form.

What hit me badly was in West Bengal when a bride is being evaluated, knowing or practicing Ravindra Sangeet is a jewel in her crown. A Bharat Natyam dancer in South is a preferred bride.

And here in my home state, Odissi dancers are assumed to be of not great characters. Unfortunately, the allegations are by Odiyas, who should be otherwise proud of the dance form and the dancers of their state.

I made three promises to myself. First, I will arrange the first ever Odissi dance program with the greatest grandeur. Second, I will work to demolish the wrong notion of character assassination of genuinly dedicated dancers and last but not least Odissi Dance must travel all over the world.

A Gujarati professional and businessman Mr Bankim Kothari, an extremely popular personality in Oman was surprisingly very fascinated and volunteered to support the dance show. He went on spending money from his pocket to make the show grand. The dance show that had 1100 viewers against seating capacity of the hall of 300 people was demonstrative of the popularity of the Dance form Odissi.

Over night, I was a celebrity having brought the most popular dance form and one among the seven classical dance forms from Odisha to Middle East. When I started planning the show I estimated a cost of about Rs 26 lacs, in present day exchange rate. Mr Bankim Kothari was generous to commit all amount that needs to be spent for a grand show. He was ready to spend all money we got some support from a close friend Raghvan Murthy, the entire money was arranged and the show was held in a grand style. My boss in Bank Muscat, Mr Ganeshan Sridhar, his ever-enthusiastic wife Chitra, both of whom are dance connoisseurs, flooded me with generous support in logistics, hospitality, and gifts to performers. A youngster from Odisha, Mr. Sanjib Swain working in the field of creativity, extended exceptional support by way of designing the brochure, setting up the stage and coordinating with publicity.

The arithmetic of hosting such a grand show with such investment from the pocket of few of us might not have been Arithmetically right.

But the hype, the recognition of Odissi Dance in Middle East and the awareness created due to the show, the mathematics of holding the show was right.

Mrs. Chitra Sridhar composed a dance "Poetry in Motion" with Odissi and Bharatnatyam which became very popular.

My identity in Middle East being from a state affected by repeated super cyclones, poverty and communal disharmony changed to being from the land of great dance form "Odissi". It was a remarkable feeling.

I continued to research and understand more of the dance form, its creators, the sacrifice of great Gurus and the present-day status.

I was immensely disappointed that such great dance form had no takers in early 2000. My strenuous journey to contribute significantly from my own hard earned money to popularize Odissi dance in various platforms all over the world was well recognized. I was immensely satisfied for my contribution during next 10 years to create a place for Odissi on the world map.

xxxxxxxxxxxxxxxxxxxxx

It was a lazy morning at my villa in Dubai on April 3rd 2011.

Villa 6, cluster 5 located overlooking both the Jumeirah Island Lakes and Dubai Marina skyline, the pool side rest area was always the best place for mental relaxation.

I had arrived back home from a visit to Kuwait for the Annual Function of Kuwait Odiya Association along with Mr Prasant Nanda who was the Chief Guest at Kuwait along with the Super Star of Odisha Mrs Mahasweta Ray.

On Mr Nanda's return flight, I had rerouted his ticket via Dubai so that he can spend some time in the new House.

I had entered the new villa few days back after its renovation to my choice. The mood was very buoyant on a lazy Sunday with India wining its Second Cricket World Cup the previous night with many anxious moments until Dhoni's firework and helicopter shots won India the much awaited world cup. Watching the match in the new large screen installed in the TV room was as good as watching in the Stadium itself.

From 2002 till 2011, I had grown from a person who was unaware of what is classical dance to a world recognized Odissi Dance promoter.

Thanks to few dedicated and innovative Gurus who taught me the finess, the beauty, the versatility, and the delicateness of Odissi Dance. In fact, I had worked for the dance as a great fan myself and my promotion of Odissi worldwide was very much talked around.

After a well-planned and elaborate breakfast Mr. Prasant Nanda came to me and wished to narrate a story.

We did discuss a few stories earlier to try as our joint second film project. Somehow, I did not get that fascination, being uncertain about its financial viability due to the massive losses I had incurred in my earlier film.

Having already won my first National Award, 6 international recognitions, 7 State Film Awards, I felt my next film must be both arithmetically and mathematically right.

Mr Prasant Nanda impulsively or strategically touched on an emotional cord of mine. The story of the journey of an Odissi Dancer was the theme of a new film story line. Having come across hundreds of struggling dancers, who had talent but no mentors, the story touched my heart instantly. That will be the first of its kind as a film on the journey of Odissi Dancers to be made in Odiya Language.

I was told that the film will be placed with a big actor and actress and probably will have a great box office potential as Mr Nanda will part all his expertise of story writing, screenplay, lyrics, music, editing and of course direction. It should be an ambitious high budget film in Odia standard. He also visualized the foreign location in the deserts of Muscat, Sultanate of Oman to do the shootings.

The project continued. Mr. Nanda roped in a creative jewel in Sri Satyabrat (Kuna) Tripathy whom I met for the first time. A gem of a talent who had the capacity to capture your body, mind and soul by his narratives, be it Sanskrit slokas, or comedy or poetry. We both immediately bonded. Only sad part was that he was a nonalcoholic, gutka(tobacco) addicted person but, he can instantly add to the kick of alcohol with his witty narratives when I drink.

Mr. Nanda and Kuna Tripathy made a few visits to Dubai and were holed up in one of my luxury apartments to complete the screenplay of upcoming film on Odissi.

My casual input on the story was very helpful giving better grasp to the story. I had one dream sequence of the film and my request was that scene must be there as part of the film.

It was supposed to be a face off of the dancer and Lord Jagannath that if The Lord is real of Sola Kala (Sixteen talents) then her prayers will be fulfilled, or else people will have faith on Lord Jagannath but not his Sola Kala.

The film was signed up with Babushan, an upcoming and promising actor. He is the son of legendary actor of yester years Mr Uttam Mohanty and Smt. Aparajita Mohanty. Aparajita madam would play a significant supporting role as screen mother of Babushhan. As the film moved from being an art film to a commercial movie, the multitalented, super child of my friend Mr Kishore Dash, Kiran, the consistent class topper, school topper, university topper from UK could not be accommodated in lead role. However, an experienced Archita Sahoo was roped in to play the main protagonist/heroine for commercial reason. Her character was of a struggling Odishi dancer who grew to be a world class performer. A challenging parallel role was to be played by already famous child star Prakruti Mishra, as her first debut adult role.

When the script was conceived, the film was aimed to cast that time superstar Anubhav Mohanty but reasons that remained as best kept secret, Babushan ended up with the role.

My only concern was Archita's presentation as an Odissi Dancer. She was, as a professional, volunteered to learn Odissi. Mr Nanda approached the well-known Odissi exponent Mrs Meera Das, founder and Guru of Gunjan Dance Academy, Cuttack, to train Archita the finer nuances of the dance so that she will look on screen very natural. Mrs Meera Das was also assigned to choreograph the entire Odissi dances in the film. She was magnanimous to agree to allow her talented students also to participate in the film in the elaborate and gorgeous group dance sequences.

One problem that suddenly cropped up was the name of the film. Mr Nanda had given a name "Mun Ekaa Baanara Pakshi" (I am a directionless bird). I somehow could not agree on the name as I found it very difficult to say in English. We had a heated argument. But somehow Mr. Nanda was in sinc after a night of discussions and the name "Thukul" (Freeze) was created.

The legendary maker in Prashant Nanda beautifully positioned the name Thukul in interval and Thukul in the end.

The film progressed fast with a January 14, 2012 release plan coinciding with Makar Sankranti.

There were exclusive shootings in deserts of Muscat, and other exotic locations in Sultanate of Oman. There were 32 cast and crew travelled to Muscat, Oman with excellent hospitality extended by "Al Nahda Resort" belonging to a close associate and one of the richest Omani of Indian origin who generously made it free of cost.

A massive set was erected by the best Art Director of Odisha, Late Budha Maharana near Bhubaneswar for the song shooting.

The Film got the reputation of being costliest film at that time.

Unfortunately, due to few unexpected incidents, the budget of the film skyrocketed, and I had to sell some investments to arrange the quick cash.

My conviction to invest was boosted by one word from Sri Prashant Nanda. "He is making it with his 100% passion and management. If the film ends in loss, I will get back my money from him and if the film makes profit it is mine". I was in Tokyo, Japan on my business assignments and was a bit hard pressed for the money. However, I never even thought about it due to my confidence on him.

The film was released with lot of fanfare, publicity and hype. I was fortunate to attend the premier at a packed Jayshree Hall at Badambadi, Cuttack.

I left India the next day. After 7days, I got a massage from Sri Nanda "I am Sorry I have failed. People have not accepted the film".

The film was distributed by his very longtime associate, the Duo of famous Jitu and Dipu (Jitu Khandelwal and Dipu Dash). Dipu Dash was the Production Manager/Designer of the film too.

Though I had noticed the lack of proper publicity, I was advised that enough is being done. After years of film making later on and getting to understand distribution a bit more, I got a feeling that the film was neither positioned nor promoted deservingly compared to the massive cost of making it.

A month later I was informed that the income from the halls was not enough for the pending publicity cost. With full trust on Sri Prashant Nanda I never asked for any accounts.

The film got sold with carpet copy rights to Taranga for Rs 17.00 lacs.

Neither me or Mr Nanda had the futuristic vision of the digital revolution that was coming.

I ended up with a loss of Rs.1.67 crores. Everyone was paid without any compromise on their agreed price but only I lost money.

I tried to compensate Mr Nanda for his genuine hard work and labor in a small way that I could.

The film went on to win Five State Awards as Best Story, Best Director, Best Cinematography, Best Make Up and Best Art Direction.

As the film was neither a film of Art nor reflecting the real Odissi Dance journey, I felt it inappropriate to send to any International Festivals.

My losses were too much to share with any one. As it is said "you cannot show your wound at a wrong place to others as you yourself can see it", I drowned myself in the fun of drinks and parties and forgot about the financial disaster the film had caused me.

The arithmetic was totally wrong and unfortunately the mathematics was also totally wrong.

Babushan became a Superstar of Odisha, so also Archita. Prakruti Mishra became a national star. I would not say they became big due to this film. May be the film gave them few notches of recognition in their future journey.

● ● ●

THE KADVISACH OF KADVIHAWA

It was a busy evening at Bhubaneswar Club. I had been to the club for a drink with a friend during one of my visits to Bhubaneswar in 2014. A great common friend and big well-wisher saw me and requested me to meet a celebrity film maker of Odisha. It was the most famous Sri Nila Madhav Panda. I was a friend on his Facebook and had many times messaged him suggesting collaboration to work together.

It was my face to face meet with him for the first time. A very charming personality, very soft-spoken, and a man of few words. I narrated the coincidence that during my flight in Emirates the day before, I saw his spectacular creation "I am Kalam". The film had already created ripples worldwide.

Seeing a film made by an Odiya in the famous Emirates's Sky view system with over 1000 movies of over 30 languages made me feel very proud.

Later in 2019, I was privileged to have three films produced by me on Emirates' Sky view which probably was a rare phenomenon. It was again a privilege to be greeted by the captain of the flight who came over and wished me when he was reported by the Crew that the producer of three films showing in Sky view is travelling in the flight.

Nila Madhav Panda or NMP as I fondly mention him, and I agreed to meet soon which was extremely positive for me.

During one of my transit flights to Dubai via Delhi from Bhubaneswar, I had five hours break in Delhi and I planned to call on him in his house at Delhi's famous Gulmohar Park. I was more keen to go to Gulmohar Park knowing that great Sri Amitabh Bachchan has a house there.

I drove from the airport with a bouquet of flowers and a rare single malt whisky. I was very warmly received by NMP and he very fondly introduced me to his wife Mrs Barnali Rath and his life, eye of the pupil, young son Aatman, fondly called Attu. They also had another family member, their very favorite dog Boske.

Nila Madhav, his wife Barnali as I called her later, his son Aatman had certain remarkable simplicity, warmth, genuineness and irresistible friendliness.

Without any formality or hesitation, he offered and I agreed to have few drinks of vodkas which is my favorite daytime drink. Maybe psychologically most alcoholic drinks are red and drank in night whereas vodka being white it doesn't make you feel guilty drinking it at daytime.

There was an exclusive starter. Very simply cut fresh fish fry with a typically homemade sauce of lemon, olive oil, garlic and chilies. The sauce was so delicious and was such an excellent combination with the fish fry that I borrowed the recipe, and it became a normal regular accompaniment in my household whenever there is a drinking session.

Few drinks and then the lunch followed. It was just not lunch but my culinary journey into eating bliss. Delicious, mind blowing authentic and a challenge to the mouth.

The trigeminal nerve stimulation, gustatory cortex, all worked to the ultimate eating experience.

My parting words to both NMP and his wife Barnali was "do they have enemies? If ever they have one, they just have to call them home to eat and they will soon become closest of friends."

NMP who was privileged to do the greatest documentary on Navakalevar 2015, was very magnanimous to offer me to participate as Coproducer. It was as good as a God sent opportunity to be of some service to Lord Jagannath. Who will not accept it without blinking an eye? I accepted the offer with my greatest gratitude.

"God's Own People" as the documentary was named, went on to be premiered at Cannes International Festival creating an awe of audience on the Human God.

On our travel to Cannes, From Delhi via Dubai, we unfortunately missed the flight as both of us got immensely engrossed on a future project.

With lot of difficulty, we could manage to reroute ourselves via Paris with a night stay and travel to Cannes next day morning.

Instead of a simple six-hour journey we ended up with almost 20 hours' journey besides higher expenses and inconvenience. We reached Paris early evening and checked into a hotel nearby. After freshening up we went down to pick up some dinner.

As Nila Madhav was not drinking in those days, I went to the ground floor to a typical English pub for a drink.

As I was alone and was enjoying the romantic feel of Paris, I was approached by a beautiful Norwegian French Air Crew. I was very pleased with her articulate behavior and knowledge of Indian History. And in no time we became friendly. NMP joined us after a while and to my greatest loss of confidence, the lady totally fell for him. I am well known as a Ladies Man. For me it was a learning that women just do not fall for style, money or position but for the intellect of a person.

Over the period, a family bonding developed with NMP, partially for excellent hospitality of exotic food but more for my interaction to learn from his vast experience and knowledge of work spread across in Italy, UK and of course in many parts of India.

During few such interactions, he revealed his concept of doing a special film which he has been working on for over 5 years and till that date he thought it to be his best concept.

During one of our great food and alcohol nights with both of us being high, I mentioned to him that how long we will be glorified by just one creative identity for both of us like "I am Kalam" for him and

"Jiaanta Bhoota" for me. I proposed that we must do something together and create a new name and fame.

We came together for a subject which in Odisha we used to hear in our early schools. *"Jala gahle srusti nash: jala bihune srusti nasa."* ("Too much water is bad for community and too less water is also bad for the community).

The concept was to show the super cyclone in Odisha and the unfortunate famines in Rajasthan.

The film was to end in one line "Global Warming and Climatic Change will affect millions of lives all around the world within next decade only."

It was enough for me to agree instantly to make the film. From the rare cyclones in Odisha in eighties and nineties, it has become a frequent in the last few years. There are many depression and cyclone warnings regularly in Bay of Bengal area.

We used to get cold and flu during season changes. Whereas now we get flu round the year. Unseasonal rains, flood and cyclones have become regular features affecting the life styles of people badly so also affecting the agriculture, the major source of income.

Global Warming and Climatic Change was not much talked of or addressed till early 2000.

NMP was very specific that the film being an art genre film, the Return on Investment was risky to predict. While no stones will be unturned to meet break-even, but much must not be expected was the conclusion.

The unprecedented world phenomenon of Covid-19 was a spine-chilling experience for the world. Nothing can be said about the cause or effect except it was a catastrophic. However, the film clearly predicted unusual phenomenon due to the effect of Global Warming and Climatic Change three years before.

Preparation for the film "**Kadvihawa**" went in full speed. With earlier pre-production work, most of the artists were already shortlisted. NMP with his experienced team of support staff was hands on with the work. In almost three months of preparations, the camera rolled out to far off deserts of Rajasthan and to the side of the Chambal River that divided Madhya Pradesh and Rajasthan.

I must salute the entire team of cast and crew who fully devoted to their work with extreme passion and commitment.

NMP who always becomes a vegetarian during film shoots was leader per excellence motivating everyone to give inputs probably double than their capacity.

The shoot got finished three days earlier than the schedule. A day saved obviously results in saving of substantial money. The post production was massive task to ensure the directors vision has been captured.

The first copy before proper BGM (Back Ground Music) and color corrections was sent by NMP to me. I could not wait till evening and immediately streamed it to my home theatre in Dubai. I was speechless with the outcome. The flow of the story, immaculate acting by Sanjay Mishra as a blind man who is always scared that his son will commit suicide under loan recovery pressure, the ruthless loan recovery officer played by Ranvir Shorey who had an unfortunate agony buried in his heart that gets reflected in his arrogant behaviour, all came out better than real.

The entire cast and crew had their blood and sweat written all over the film.

NMP took almost 4 months to carefully supervise the BGM and other technical finishing.

That year, India's entry for Oscar was the film 'Newton' made by a highly successful professional financial person based out of Nigeria Mr Manish Mundra of Drishyam Films.

Nila Madhab was well acquainted with him earlier. Mr Mundra was very appreciative of the film and proposed to come in as a producer. He agreed to navigate the film towards theatrical release due to his vast experience.

With a lot of effort by everyone, an exceptional Trailer was made. On release of the trailer, it became highly popular reaching over 15 million views.

The film was released in November. Despite extraordinary efforts by NMP, the film could not get the audience to theaters.

The film went to over 30 International Film Festivals and was the talk of the festivals due to its explosive subject.

The film won the 64th National Award under Special Mention category.

It did not get the desired arithmetic result. But the social awareness it created besides the awards and nominations both in India and internationally, it definitely was a great mathematical success.

(National Award from President of India Sri Pranab Mukherjee)

The Film created an invaluable bond between NMP and myself. In spite of being much younger, he almost became a mentor to me and guided me in my celluloid journey. I was always positioned close to him which also gave me high positive acceptance in the political circle where he was significantly associated with. I got acquainted with top level political, bureaucratic and business people as well. My soft nature, candid views and helping nature made me likable, appreciated and respected. I would not hesitate to accept to have got visibility both in political circles as well as film circles with his association.

The mathematical benefit that I got out of the association with Nila Madhav impossible to calculate.

● ● ●

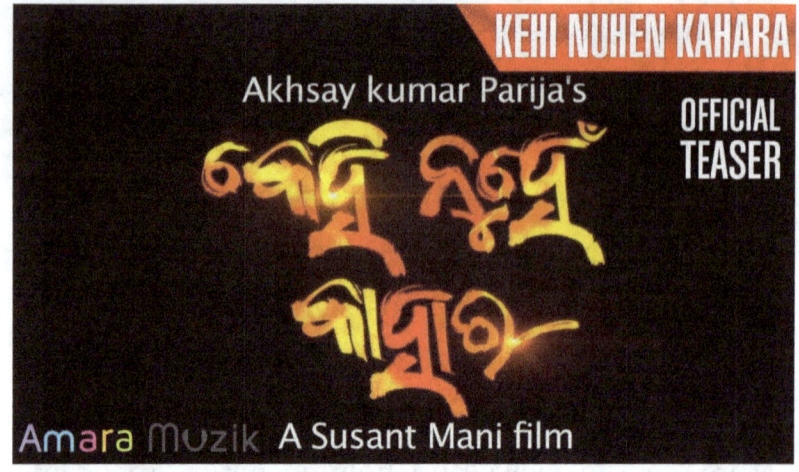

BIG DREAM WENT SOWER!!

I was at home on a lazy afternoon on a Friday which was a weekend off in Dubai. Lunch was few cans of beer, sumptuous home cooked food by the Odiya cook of Rohi Fish curry, Patato Paste (Aloo Bharta), Ilish fish cooked with Mustard oil and curd, mung daal and double boiled rice (Usuna Bhata). A bit of overating closes your eyes for an afternoon siesta.

As I woke up by 4 pm and there was nothing to do, I put on the TV and went to Odiya channels thru Dish TV to see news in Odisha. Few savvy enterprising people were managing to smuggle in and install Dish TV which is supposed to be banned in UAE.

However, while channel hopping, I came across one interesting scene of two beautiful known faces that prompted me to stop there. It was a Film going on the Screen with a handsome boy and beautiful girl singing a very sensitive song. The lyrics, music and scene depiction was heart touching. It immensely touched my heart with the lyric being "Time please go slow" (Tu dhire dhire chal Samay).

It was the Thukool hero and heroine, Babushan and Archita.

The film's execution was impressive, logical and I could see a directorial efficiency in the making of the film with two fairly newcomers acting so well.

Both the Protagonists of Babushan and Archita had already acted in my film Thukool directed by Prasanta Nanda. Their personal dedication, hard work and commitments were unquestionable irrespective of the Financial result of the Film. Reportedly they were not on good terms during shooting of the film Thookul, but neither the director nor me had any complaint about their personal equation but their onscene chemistry was immaculate.

After my two films, where Financial Arithmetic had gone wrong significantly, irrespective of National Awards and one dozen State Awards, I had almost given up on Odiya films. I was venturing into Hindi Films by that time.

The moment I completed seeing the end of the film named "Chocolate", I called the Production Manager of AKP Group and inquired about Susant Mani, the director of the Film, Chocolate and his telephone number.

I was impressed by the director's work, the framing of the shots, the detailing, the flawlessness, and over all look on the screen.

I picked up the phone and made a call to Susant Mani. He was obviously surprised. Irrespective of doing only two Films, I was already well known in Odisha. It was due to the first International Visibility of "The Living Ghost" almost in about 12 Countries globally and winning 6 international awards. Subsequently it won the National Award in National Category not in regional film category.

Thukool made its splash due to its songs, Odishi dance and being the costliest film at that time that included foreign locations and shootings.

My question to Sushant Mani was "can he do another film like "Chocolate". I am sure he was caught off guard but in his normal humble way he opined that "yes he could". I liked his silent confidence.

We met in March 2015 in Bhubaneswar. Contrary to my expectations, Susant Mani turned out to be an extremely decent, shy and a humble person.

After the unfortunate arithmetic of my earlier films, I tried my best to learn film making. I attended few classes including New York Film Institute's 5 days' workshop at Abu Dhabi besides interaction with many Directors of films in Odisha and across India.

Susanta Mani gave a budget of Rs.60 lacs to make a film with condition that if not better but equivalent of a film like Chocolate will be made.

Earlier year, Chocolate was also competing along with Thukool in State Film Award. Thukool bagged Best Story, Best Director to Prasanta Nanda and Three other category of Best Art Director, Best Make up and Best Editing. Had I been a judge, probably, I would have made few changes in favor of Chocolate. I was told later that the story line was a bit similar to some other language film and hence best film and best directions eluded Susant Mani.

Next step to venture a film with Susant Mani was to select an appropriate story.

Prasant Nanda in whose name the story of Thukool was credited informally conveyed my role on the original story on Odishi Dance. As a result, I was honored with receiving the Best Story Award on stage from the Hon. Governor of Odisha.

I was very much moved by a film at that time in 2014 making waves. It was "Kahani" of Sujay Ghosh, brilliantly enacted by Vidya Balan. I wished a story on those lines, where the mystery has to be beyond guess. I had my ever-unforgettable mystery play "Mousetrap" in back of my mind and we developed the theme of a murder mystery with murderer to be beyond guess.

Susant Mani very genuinely gave the credit of story to me in the film. He along with his associates developed the screen play in their usual way of vanishing into jungle for a week. They just carry some rice, vegetables, and a pressure cooker. They eat some rice and daal or khichdi and fully concentrate on the screen play.

Susant Mani, in spite of being a great director is not very eloquent story teller. He used his Associate Mr Dilip Choudhary who narrated me the screenplay during my next visit to Bhubaneswar from Dubai.

His narration was fascinating, especially the creation of a court scene where, in spite of all evidences of the suspected murderer including the murder video, he was proved innocent. Later, after the film was released many critics told me that wish the Court scene that was enacted by Late Sri Bijay Mohanty Vs Sri Kuna Tripathy could have been longer as it was gripping and enjoyable.

Having locked the story and screen play, it was the star cast challenge. I had special preference for Sri Kuna Tripathy as he was already well known as a versatile actor to enact a challenging role of a lawyer who had never lost a case.

The story always raised a finger on him to be the main culprit.

Kuna, as I call him as a younger brother by now, had to put up a new get up of Long Hair, gotee beard and no pan parag eating which was a punishment for him during the shoots.

In an audition of potential heroines, considered rather as Hero of the film, Miss Abahani Vidyadhar, Miss Elina Samantray emerged as a natural choice.

Already one film old, she had the spark in her to play the mysterious Abahani Vidyadhar from Hongkong, who lands in Odisha to investigate her father's death.

Later after release of the film, a stylish imitation of young girls in Odisha was "I am Abahani Vidyadhar from HongKong. What others cannot do I can do."

There was another shortlisted actor who could have given a fight to Elina, absented herself being misguided by someone from the film industry.

But she never got the chance till date to be a powerful Protagonist by the Film industry.

Susanta Mani chose the male Protagonist which later turned out to be unacceptable to the audience.

His biggest catch was to convince the legend Sidhant Mohapatra to do an extremely powerful role.

Mr Ratikant Satapathy sang the song of "Mane pade sehi pila dina". It was as beautiful as the "Tu Dhir Dhir Chale Samay" of Chocolate. The song won the Best Lyrics award, but I would have been happier had it won the Best Singer Award too.

Odisha State Best Film Award
(Mohan Sundar Dev Goswami Award for Best Film)

The making of the film progressed with full speed. As usual I do not attend shootings leaving it to the full independence and control of the Director.

After the first edit review, I did find quite a bit of logical lapses. As the soul of the story was already in my heart, I had to request few reshoots. The film got completed with very encouraging compliments from the Censor Board.

As a first step, I requested and agreed by the connoisseur of Odisha Event Management Scene, Sri Satyabrata (Sanu) Rath of Prelude Communications to market the film. He came with the idea of a professional publicity campaign on par with Bollywood. A high decibel campaign was launched along with brilliant trailers and teasers made by Susant Mani.

Certain things in life are less said the better.

We could not crack a deal with Tarang channel to present the film and distribute it.

Their CFO, a noted professional, quoted a price that was insulting for the film which was made with enhanced cost of Rs 72.00 lakhs and publicity budget of Rs.32.00 lakhs.

A common friend took me to a distribution house with an excellent pedigree. Unfortunately, the key person of the distribution house went on vacation and returned one day before the film release. I still got a strong feeling that he wished the film to fail. Could be professional rivalry. The gentleman who till date continues to be 'big talk low performance' is good at criticism but poor at highlighting the positives.

The publicity of the film was remarkable and new kind in Odisha Cine World. I think I still could not pay few lakhs to Mr Sanu Rath and probably being an extraordinarily decent person he never asked knowing the fate of money collection for the film.

The film could not be released in as many halls as expected. The box office report was disastrous. Distribution was an area, where I had no knowledge. Later on, I realized it is more important for an Odia film to reach the audience nearby than the audience travelling long distance to see a film. Obviously their choice will be to see Hindi films.

The first show for elites of Bhubaneswar witnessed tremendous appreciation.

The informal announcement of "Guess the Murderer" by interval, to win a scooter, had no successful takers. Only the veteran, Ms Annu Choudhary could guess the suspense and told so in my ears No wonder with over 40 films as heroine and with her experience she could guess the mystery right.

Susant Mani sent me an emotional message that he is sorry for such huge losses. I told him that I will give him one more chance like the Raj Kapoor's Mera Nam Joker and Bobby.

He did make one more film for me "Love you Jessica "which was a low budget film but had no takers for distribution.

"Kehi Nehuen Kahar" name was chosen by me as per the story line where no one can be trusted.

However, in Odisha, especially in Cineworld the name became synonymous for the rampart selfishness, cheating, insecurity and trust deficit.

Kehi Nuhe Kahar created record in State Film Award function winning the Mohan Sundar Dev Goswami Award for the Best film, probably the first commercial film winning the award over quite good Art films. The Jury definitely saw the original story, the making, and all other parameters. The film won 7 State Awards, almost equally won record of seven state awards for Jiaanta Bhoota.

The Arithmetic went terribly wrong but the Mathematics was right.

NB: Susant Mani directed for me the biggest ever TV Serial of Odisha "Kemiti Kahibi Kaha", a record in Odisha Television history starring Sidhant Mohapatra in television. He also directed the hugely Popular OTT Cinema "Chocolate 2".

He directed my recent Film "Drustikona" where I experimented again my own writing besides significantly contributing on the screenplay.

I would assume with "Kemiti Kahibi Kaha" for over 10 months, he almost was churning out 5 films a month and over the period it was almost 50 films. My simple arithmetic is he made 6,760 minutes of final content. If a full length feature film is of 2 hours and 15 minute or 135 minutes' duration it translates to 50 films. With the Superstar of Odisha as Protagonist and the most popular heroine in Supriya and many other celluloid stars, it was not a series but mega movies. The arithmetic of Kemiti Kahibi Kaha went terribly wrong with massive losses. I still have to pay the last month remuneration of Susant Mani. Magnanimously he had never asked me nor reminded me. I have never defaulted to any one for their payment dues and hopefully I will clear his dues soon.

● ● ●

TRUST AND DESTINY

It was mid May 2015. I got a call from India on my Dubai mobile. The number was attractive. Presuming it must be a VIP, I picked up the call. It was a very warm and pleasant voice with a visible familiarity on the conversation. It was the superstar of Odisha. Ms Barsha Priyadarshini, newly married and a household name in Odisha. When she introduced me herself, I humbly replied that it is not necessary. I had not still seen many Odia films but who would not know her, especially with her recent marriage to the superstar of Odisha, Anubhav Mohanty.

She was fascinated with a story of Dr Pratibha Ray, who I always referred as the next Goddess of knowledge in Odisha after Maa Saraswati.

Barsha was very spontaneous and talked quite many things in our first interaction over phone

The book she dreamed to make film was Shilapadma, a highly fascinating story by Dr Pratibha Ray.

I promised to contact her next week as I was already scheduled to visit Odisha few days later. I was also honored with a call from Mr Anubhav Mohanty who was already a member of Parliament, Rajya Sabha.

Our planned meeting with Anubhav and Barsha could not take place, as it was a touch and go due to my more important engagement and their delayed arrival due to unavoidable reasons. I apologized in the night promising to catch up some other time soon.

I made enquiries on the story of Shilapadma and the budget needed to make it into a film but got feedback that to do justice to the book, at least Rs.10 crores will be the expenses. I personally decided myself to be not into the project based on its uncertain financial viability.

Irrespective of the project, I was very much ready for my next film. I wished to go back to Odisha history for my next film.

From the childhood two characters from Kalinga, now Odisha, always made a place in the hearts of Odiyas for their glory. Samrat Kharavela and Buxi

Jagabandhu. I was aware that a historical film will obviously cost much more than a commercial film.

I read few books on Samart Kharavel so also books on Buxi Jagabandhu.

My best reading time of books, which I love, was always airport lounges and long flights that I had to undertake for my business. The flights could be as long as 16 hours to transatlantic or 18/20 hours to Australia/New Zealand.

During a flight from Delhi to Dallas, USA, where in my as usual first stop after immigration and security was the Book Shop. I came across a book by Dr Subhrakant Behera named 'The Unfortunate Celebrity: the life and time of Buxi Jagabandhu.' It was like a lottery for me and next 6 hours was reading delight coming across incidents in life of Buxi Jagabandhu during the famous Paika Revolution (Paika Bidroha). The book was like a movie you don't read but you just visualize it. While reading, I resolved to connect with him on arrival at Dallas USA for assistance and guidance.

But alas, arriving in USA and after google search of his details, I realized that he was no more. An eminent Indian Foreign Service Officer (IFS), he had succumbed to a heart attack in Australia.

After reading the book in detail, I got fascinated to further progress on making a film on Paika Bidroh which was led by Buxi Jagabandhu.

After returning to Dubai, I called superstar of Odisha Sri Anubhav Mohanty and I could visual a Buxi Jagabandhu in him.

We fixed a meeting at Hotel Pramod at Cuttack at 5 pm on a specific day and was there sharp at 5 pm as per my regular habit. I was amazed to find Anubhav reaching sharp 5 pm that too in a track suit. Later it was revealed that giving respect to my firm discipline, he come on a bike at Cuttack to avoid the loss time in congested Cuttack traffic in a car.

Anubhav was already fascinated for Buxi Jagabandhu and had a hint from Mr Manmath Behera. Manmath was an upcoming story and screenplay writer. He lifted the TRP of my Serial "Sahanai" in Tarang Channel significantly on his own by tweaking the story, editing screenplay and took it to a different tangent, the fantasy zone. The show which was on ventilator took off to the highest TRP. I had and still have lots of respect for his creativity.

There was nothing that would have raised any hesitation for Anubhav. Few more meetings and we decided on going ahead with Buxi Jagabandhu and Paika Bidroh.

The story went to screenplay board when my research revealed that 2017 is going to be the 200 years of Paika Bidroh which took place in the year 1817.

My further research revealed that "Paika Bidroh" of 1817 was actually the first war of Indian Independence, the armed fight 40 years before the famous Sepoy Mutiny.

Nobody in Odisha was aware of this fact of Paika Bidroh being the first war of independence.

The East India Company's British Rulers were surprised that the small state in Coastal East was still not surrendering to their colonialism. They did all treachery to annex the then Odisha to the growing British rule.

They found the biggest uniting force of Odiyas was the unlimited faith in Lord Jaganath. The entire Odiya community all over world even today is united due to their faith in Lord Jaganath. So they insulted Lord's perceived Representative, the King of Khordha. It did not affect people's faith on Lord Jaganath, rather it was counterproductive that it united the people more.

They demonetized "Kaudi", the currency that was prevalent for centuries, and banned harvesting of salt at Chilika Lake, a way of hitting below the belt. They failed. Hunger did not suppress people.

Last was decommissioning the Paikas from Army. It was done under the pretext that they are no more needed with their traditional weapons of sword, arrows etc. Instead, British will bring in new trained soldiers trained in Guns and other artillery weapons.

The ever warrior community known all over India and spread to Sri Lanka for their bravery were decommissioned on the pretext of firepower of arms and ammunition that will replace traditional arms of swords, spears etc.

This was an insult to the self-esteem of Paikas. A Paika could starve till death or may be sick but is emotionally ready to fight a war till their last breath.

And what happened was unprecedented.

Unlike Sepoy Mutiny of 1857, where rebels lost out, in Paika Bidroha, 2017 the British could not win.

Rebels fought for 10 years and British was forced to make a compromise. A truce.

I got a feeling from inside my heart that either the revolution was deliberately hidden from the pages of history to save the British Empire from insult and humiliation in front of the world or there were no known Odiya historians in 1817 who could have documented it.

I took a humble resolve in my small way. I will make the film and bring the truth to public knowledge.

Lacs of soldiers were brutally killed, and their bodies were eaten away by wild animals. Their final rites could not be done for 12 years in the absence of body for the ceremonial cremation. Their wives remain married women, though in their heart they knew they have been widowed. Their warrior and beloved Paika Husbands will not come back. Their children waited for their brave father to return. Small children took to learning Paika fighting skills to avenge the inhuman treatment meted out to the fighting Paika fathers.

I did not remember THESE ASPECTS OF AGONY WAS EVER DISCUSSED ON ANY PLATFORM, DEBATE OR DISCUSSIONS in Odisha.

By now, Satyabrata (Sanu) Rath of Prelude who did a remarkable campaign of my earlier film Kehi Nunen Kahar had become like a younger brother.

Sanu planned a spectacular but intellectual launch of Buxi Jgabandhu, The hero of Paika Bidroha.

On January 11, 2016 Anubhav completed 11 years of his celluloid Career and rose to become the No 1 hero of Odisha. He requested a path breaking film like Buxi & Paika Bidroha to be launched on 11 th January.

Sanu and his team worked day and night to give a spectacular surprise to Odisha. Sanu personally worked till wee hours to give final touches to all audio visual and creative details. He did not take immense trouble just to host it for business but because he was fascinated. Most of the work, I found later part in life, he does excellent when he is fascinated without bothering on economics.

Nothing was revealed what was the function for. A very attractive invitation card was made with only the text that "Please attend to witness history unfolding and be part of the history".

The launch of Buxi Jagabandhu, the Unsung hero of Paika Bidroha was spectacular.

Every important personality was there. Present was Hon Minister of Govt of Odisha, Sri Ashok

Panda, Sri Biswa Bhushan Harichandan who later adorned the Governorship of Andhra Pradesh and Chhattisgarh, Hon MP and Literate Sri Prasana Patasani, many members of Legislative Assembly and Parliament, and most of the celluloid glitterati from the Ollywood.

The Banquet Hall at Hotel Crown got overcrowded. The response for the news of making such a film was unanimously appreciated by Television, media, politicians, bureaucracy, and filmdom. Social media was not as prominent in those days. Still there were enough flashes in prevalent social media.

We had not announced the Director of the film yet. The major question during the Press briefing was the proposed Director. I managed to avoid naming the proposed Director with lots of pretentions. The fact was we still had not finalized the Director.

It was overwhelming to observe the voluntary assurance of help and support from writers, poets, historians, media world and many intellectuals.

The biggest complement was from the Paika Community of Khorda belt, who came in many numbers and blessed me for having taken such a step.

Among all the celebrations and research work, I got a call from a close friend from press, Sri Ashok Palit to call Sri Manmohan Mohapatra.

xxxxxxxxxxxxxxx

The encyclopedia of information on film related subjects, Sri Ashok Palit, after many a time request and persuasions, took me to the house of Sri Manmohan Mohapatra few months back. In my heart of heart, I was longing to meet him for past 10 years. Here I was sitting in front of him, the 9-time President Award Winner, a gold medalist alumnu of FTII, Pune and the new trend setter of Odiya films. I would rather be happy to say that thru his films, he gave Odiya cinema an identity in National and International level.

I had rarely seen such a humble but charming personality like Manmohan Babu in my long diversified career.

We hit an instant chord. I was bought into him. I later came to know that he was also sold into me. My respect was for his unfathomable talent. His instant liking of me, probably was undeserving on my part. I wonder if I have any quality that could impress a legend like him. Sri Ashok Palit told me to call Mr Mohapatra at 11.43 am India time next day.

I called him 11.43 am as suggested. He is well known for his astrological affiliation. Manmohan babu, in his humble manner conveyed that he himself being of Paika Pedigree, was very excited to know such a film is being planned. Very surprising to me and to my utmost honor, he volunteered to help for making of the film in whatever way he can.

I sat down calmly for few minutes yet to digest what I listened and in what way I could get his association.

When the proposed film was announced, we had not revealed the name of director. The process of choosing a good director was on but not finalized.

A nine-time National Award winner, creator of new age Cinema in Odisha and like a fool I was thinking what help he can offer?

He should be the director for such a revolutionary film!!

Though it was a working day and I was in office, my Executive Secretary, Isha, a mother and sister figure for all my matters, arranged my travel bag to office and I straight drove to airport for Odisha in next thirty minutes.

I was aware about Manmohan Babu's prolonged sickness though not in detail. It would a great personal achievement to make a film with him as director.

I booked a flight on Emirates, the one earliest available. I found a flight in next two hours. Contrary to international flights requirement, where one should reach airport 3 hours before, I had no worry being a Platinum Member on Emirates. Dubai airport also has special check in and immigration facility for First/Business Class passengers in a separate building, I was sure to board the flight. My excitement of working with him was only in my mind.

I called Mr. Ashok Palit after settling down in Emirates first class lounge and gulped down few shots of classic Vodka martini. I enquired about the health of Manmohan Babu. First, I came to know that he was bedridden for over 12 years and has not made any film except a film by his son in Hindi. But it was not completed.

Mr Ashok Palit agreed to my suggestion that Manmohan babu will be the best choice to direct Buxi and Paika Bidroha.

Reaching Odisha appeared a bit long this time due to the tension. I drove to Manmohan babu's house directly from the airport.

I spoke to him straight that it will be my privilege to have him direct the film. I told him the truth that my first choice was Mr Prasant Nanda who had already politely declined.

I have not yet been able to finalize someone who I feel can deliver.

He was a bit hesitant on the ground that can he do justice to such a venture which he had never done before. He was also concerned for his health. Ashok Babu put Ghee in Manmohan babu's Creative desire. If he hires a great team of assistants, he can easily make it. I was not prepared to listen a "no", I left requesting him to think over for a day and respond.

He responded by next morning itself. That If I feel confident, he will give it a try leaving the rest to God. His requirement was to meet immediately Anubhav, his creative team and few other potential assistants.

Like me, Anubhav also went into 7 th heaven. When I enquired with him whether he is in consent with me for Manmohan babu to direct the film, he humbly said he is speechless. I gave him the next difficult challenge that Manmohan babu wants to meet him and his team next morning at 8 am.

Anubhav who himself admits that he is very poor in his time management and a late riser, instantly agreed that he will be there at 8am. His comment was if he would have been told to come at 6 am he would have made it too.

Anubhav reached on dot. I was decoding in my mind that Manmohan babu's consent after 12 hours at 8 pm and next meeting at 8 am must be the alignment with his astrological beliefs.

After all of us mesmerizingly listened Manmohan Babu narrate few of the great film making formulas, Anubhav while touching Manmohan Babu's feet, made a statement "till date, I was thinking I know acting and film making, if not masters but at least matriculation. Today, I realized I am a zero. Yet to start learning".

A very simple cinematic and cinematographic narration given by Manmohan babu that day, became a religion for me and Anubhav in all our next films.

The biggest but complex work was to identify CG or VFX specialists as the film has to have significant CG work. Computer Graphic or CG and VFX has become an extremely acceptable as well as convenient mechanism to make films without erection of large shooting sets.

As a layman in cinema technology, visual effects is the process in which imagery is created or manipulated outside the context of a live action shot. The integration of live action footage and another Live action footage or CG to create realistic imagery is called VFX.

All I understood was major part of the film will be shot on a blue mat and the scenes will be recreated with CG and VFX.

Some significant amount was spent for few small but important scenes in Thukul using CG technology, but it was very insignificant and did not make any impact on the success of the film. Mr Nanda tried the new experiment that further added to the rescaled costs.

Audience became aware of CG/VFX films after Bahubali, the monumental film ever made in cinematic history of India.

I proposed and very enthusiastically agreed by Manmohan Babu was to connect Sri V Srinivas Mohan, who created Babhubali one to assist or advice. Mr Srinivas Mohan had won three President Awards for his VFX or special effects work. Since he was not doing Bahubali 2, he himself or his office was contacted.

There was immediate warm response from Mr Srinivas to work as it will be with Manmohan Babu.

The Oscar winning Sound Designer Mr Rasool Pookutty was contacted. After an elaborate discussion with Manmohan Babu, he got fascinated to work for the project. He opted that during all the shootings he will be in Odisha. He was excited to record the sound of Paika's walking in the night on dry leaves in jungle or the sound of the making of traditional weapons like swords, spears etc in a blacksmith's workshop so that British spies will not hear the metals sound. Manmohan Babu revealed that he will merge it with the temple drums and bells (ghanta and ghanti) besides the kirtan (a mass prayer) so both the sounds to synchronise rhythmically creating confusion on ears and not attracting attention of British spies.

I come across Ashutosh, Manmohan Babu's eldest son. He was trying to be Film director living in Mumbai. He was supposed to have a larger ambition which is possible any in Bollywood.

In spite of Manmohan Babu's hesitance in clear terms not to deal with his eldest son Asutosh, I was very impressed with his knowledge level, skill of talking, and acquaintances level of film celebrities across India. Any celebrity in films, he would be conversant and many of them he called as uncle.

In Odisha, "culture of name dropping" is very common and people take the name of an acquaintance very easily even where it not's necessary.

People who are well connected would be very discreet about their connections. However, there are many who are not so closely connected but misutilse the acquaintances.

There are people who will call "such as such" universally as "Bhai (brother) to any well-known person or if the personality is elderly then 'uncle' or mamun. I always wondered why one can't mention Mr such and such instead of these artificial addresses.

I assume mostly it may be out of respect and very few may be to show off close acquaintance.

Ashutosh's dropping names or the address of "Uncle" was mostly out of respect. His acquaintance with the cine fraternity are obviously derived for his father's extraordinary reach, acceptance and appreciation across India.

He reflected confidence in his acquaintances of celebrities and took the responsibility of connecting Mr Rasool Pookuty. We were still undecided on other team members for editing, special action and cinematography.

He almost put a gun on my head without giving me time to think or examine for the selection of Editor, Action Director etc. He always quoted if I don't pay within hours we will miss them to participate in the project.

I was reminded many a time that, most are on a significantly reduced cost for their appreciation of Manmohan Babu and opportunity to work with him.

I cannot vouch whether he actually communicated with the top and respected names as I had no evidence of it.

However, Manmohan Babu always will share that these celebrities are fascinated with the subject and the way the film is conceived by the director.

Within 24 hours, he made me part with Rs 48 lacs to the action and camera team and maybe to VFX team. He made me remit Rs 5.00 lacs to an account supposed to be the agency for Mr Rasool. He also demanded Rs.2.50 lacs for his own travel etc. which I paid.

He neither took receipt nor made a contract nor the terms of work or in case of the project not materializing the terms of refund. However, all money went in specific bank accounts.

After finalizing the team, it turned out to be a team of 24 National Award Winners with Manmohan Babu's nine awards. I jokingly added to say 25 National Award Winners as the person involved in the project, that's being me, having awarded National Award for Jiaanta Bhoota

The film project got hyped due to the team of makers who have made name and fame for themselves not only in India but around the world also.

The significant reason for the project getting attention was "Paika Bidroh", being the first war of Independence. It became a matter of pride for most Odiyas.

Before team went into completing the screenplay of the film, it got attention of many intellectuals and elderly people of Paika community in Khordha belt.

A debate got reopened as to the veracity of which is the first war of Independence. Was it Paika Bidroh of 1817 or Sepoy Mutiny of 1857.

The state Govt. of Odisha was very interested to participate in the project. We got message from the Government to discuss collaboration and support.

I did approach Central Government also looking for support.

With the encouragement the project received, came the bad news that after making all pragmatic calculations, the expected budget could be as high as Rs 7.5 crores against my expectations of Rs 2.5 crores.

A super success film in Odisha is expected to make a maximum of about Rs 2.00 crores net after all expenses of theaters and release costs.

For the film, a budget of 7.00 crores is very high and impossible to recover. However, the film will be a document for the State and to be preserved for next 100 years.

Govt of India announced a special budget in 2016 budget of about Rs 70 crores for preservation of history of Paika Bidroha. A highway was declared to be named after Buxi costing probably about Rs 1100 crores. A special memorial got planned to be built at Barunei hills with Rs 100 plus crores. But there were neither any emotion or passion to support about Rs 3.5 crores to support me to make the film.

Ashutosh forced me to part with about Rs.60.00 lacs and almost Rs 40 lacs was spent on Pre-production.

Not going into my financial losses and mental agony, Manmohan Babu and myself agreed to not go ahead with the project unless we get some Governmental support.

Some dreams are not destined to be fulfilled and the film remained a distant dream.

Mathematics was right but arithmetic could have gone terribly wrong.

● ● ●

THE WET HEAVENS

The failure to mount the ambitious Paika Bidroh project left both myself and Manmohan Babu a slumber.

Over the period of three years, I developed an excellent bonding with Manmohan Babu. I got addicted to his parting of knowledge on film making. I would call on him without fail on my visits to Odisha. We will share the aromatic Darjeeling red tea. A nondrinker of tea or coffee I started developing the taste of Red Tea with specific and unique aroma. It would extend over few hours and on one occasion it went up to six hours-to the tension and anxiety of his family members. Of course, periodic serving of red tea and local savories by family members kept us afresh and engaged.

In one of the afternoon meetings, I inquired about his selection process of good stories. With so many National Awards, it goes beyond doubt that his subject or story selection was definitely most sensitive and successful.

He was very candid in admitting that few stories have remained his dream to see the light of the day thru the camera.

One such story very dearer to his heart was 'Bhija Matira Swapna'. He strongly related to the subject of being of rural/semi urban life thru the growing stage of urbanization.

It also related to the bonding and emotional interdependence of elderly people post retirement. Ambitions get suppressed, dreams get shattered and desires have no value.

The subject fascinated me immensely having witnessed many such real life instances with retired people in my village.

I remember one gentleman from our village came back retired from a factory in Kolkata at the age of 60. When I had seen him a year earlier, he was with high youthful energy. He was a complete destruction a year after on retirement. Savings were neither a practice nor the income in Kolkata was adequate for future requirements. He appeared only waiting to get more and more aged and ultimately die.

Manmohan babu had not made a film probably during past 14 years. His good height of 6 feet plus was an enemy for his directional activity. He was a person who gets fully engaged with camera by bending down. Unlike the digital revolution these days, good directors will spend hours looking thru the camera to get the right shots. One day jokingly he commented that life of a film maker has become easy with digital camera and color correction technology. His spine gave up on the stress of hard work those days to churn out the best. He was a director of integrity. He will take the best shot irrespective of the hard work or expenses or even shooting schedules.

He was a famous Dunhill cigarette chain smoker. I have only heard about it. The stress of converting extraordinary creativity to reels strongly worked against him.

Thus Manmohan babu was bed ridden for over 14 years. Just before my unfortunately aborted Paika

Bidroh endeavor, he had recovered a lot and was able to move. That's how he could give time and effort to make Paika Bidroh.

I observed him getting rejuvenated and energetic when he is working. I think any creative person forgets his or her sickness or pain and gets energized the moment they get a chance to work in their field of passion.

I felt that if he can make a film, he may continue to be creatively engaged. I requested him to start making the film with the subject of his passion. He was a bit unsure whether it is right time to invest the kind of money in an art film where returns are doubtful. Even his forte of awards and recognition have become uncertain with a bit of infringement of politics into the world of creativity. Early days 90% of genuine makers will be going to people of influence. However, in present days the process is said to be reversed with 10% going to extraordinary talents which cannot be ignored and 90% going to people with propelled campaigns.

He was candid in his comments as to why I should be spending quite a bit of money neither with assurance of a return or any great recognition. It was difficult on my part to confide that the purpose was neither. I only wished that he starts working. I took the liberty of telling him that I don't wish to see him as the same as Raghu of Cuttack Dahibara Aludam. Raghu, the crafted food maker had been serving people for probably over 60 years and had not even thought of any innovations or expansions. Contrary, Manmohan Babu is the Property of Odisha and all Odiyas. He is not just father of his children or a property of his family and relatives. He requires to impart his God given knowledge to Odiyas.

Manmohan babu got very moved and excited. He immediately not only agreed to do the film but he also planned to start mentoring new makers who ever was interested in learning. His only request was he cannot finish the film in 15days but require few months to finish. It was more for his health conditions. I requested him to forget the cost and only focus on his work.

His style of film making which I observed and learned is to convert his mental concepts to reality thru segmented shooting. He will plan his shoots based on his mood, climate, location or actor's availability. It's like if the climate is cloudy and he intends to catch the rainbow, he will wait the full day to capture the scene. He had the unique talent of shooting scenes from his mind and finally connecting them and giving it the soul. The films always come out as splendid. I am at a loss whether I am being able to narrate his film making methods accurately.

I requested Manmohan babu to go ahead without bothering the days of shoot nor the economics. His younger son assisted him in managing the shoot. He had his usual team of Nandalal babu as writer and Dilip babu as Director of Photography. Dilip babu had been his Cinematographer for most of his films. Once Manmohan babu confided in me that Dilip babu can do a shoot accurately even without being told. He can read Manmohan babu's mind. I left the star cast to him as I was not very conversant of the story line. It would have been an insult to ask to such level of a film maker. He only confided in me that the lady protagonist has been changed from the highly talented Lipsa Mishra to the most natural actress Gargi Mohanty. The male protagonist was a new comer with Mr Mihir Das playing a challenging role.

The film got finished in about three months. Manmohan babu did editing himself and the first cut was presented to me during one of my visits to India. I was overwhelmed by the acting of Mr Mihir Das and Ms Gargi Mohanty. I called Mr Das and congratulated him for his spectacular performance as a retired old widower living alone. I told him also that nobody can take away the best actor award from him in the next State Award. There was a slight change in name from Bhija Matira Swapna (Dreams of Wet Soil) to Bhija Matira Swarg (Wet Heavens).

After Censors, the film entered the National Award competition in February 2019. The film also in due course entered the State Film Awards Competition. The film went to Berlin International Festival, Venice International Festival and Karlovy Vary International Film Festival. The realistic subject, the cinematography and direction created extensive buzz. For reasons of extraordinary growth of number of films competing, and qualitative growth of films made around world, our film could not make it to the final selection.

It narrowly missed National Award due to certain interference of a big anti Man Mohan babu lobby and the Odiyas pulling down Odiyas syndrome which I would like to forget.

The film practically made a sweep in the State Film Awards 2018, winning six Awards in the Category of Best Film (Mohan Sunder Dev Goswami Award), Best Direction, Best Actor for Mr Mihir Das, Best Cinematography for Mr Dilip Ray, Best Screenplay and Best Dialogue. With

Best Film Award for Bhija Matira Swarga

this award, I equalled the maximum Best Film Awards with Manmohan Babu himself who was the highest number of Best Film Award winner earlier.

During the Award Function an elderly gentleman who was an ace Cinematographer in Mumbai of high repute confided in me that irrespective of being a much acclaimed DOP, he would like to salute the work of Mr Dilip Ray in the film. That's professional magnanimity unlike the poor jealousy prevalent in Odisha.

Proudly holding his trophy of Best Actor for the first time in life Mr Mihir Das straight came to me avoiding the hounding media and told one line in my ears. 'I want to do more with you and this is what I always dream for'. My misfortune he did not live longer to bigger journey of both of us.

Manmohan babu was rejuvenated and motivated. He was ready for the next. He had a storyline troubling him for over 30 years. He confessed to me that the story line troubles him even in his dreams. It was a simple story of shattered dreams of a common man. Story of a principled bureaucrat finding himself in receiving end being unable to save people from the unfortunate laws of land which was outdated written decades back.

We moved forward to make the film. He got his spirit to work. His health problems continued but he was facing it like a brave man.

Manmohan Babu was hospitalized for some breathing complicity. At 4 PM in hospital, quite energetic, he asked his son to bring some papers and pen as he already visualized the last scene of the film.

At 5 PM he was no more!!!!

My first film with him became his last film.

Few days later he was conferred the prestigious Padmashree Award but he was not there to receive.

As I write this memoir, he remains the only Odiya Film personality from Odisha to be conferred the glorious Padmashree.

I will be naive to even think arithmetic or mathematics of my association with such a great man.

With tears in eyes, I can only say Manmohan Babu and NMP still remain the SUN who enlighten me as a Moon to reflect light.

● ● ●

THE NEW CHALLENGE OF COPY FILM

With unexpected delays and uncertainties in making of Paika Bidroh, Anubhav and myself went into depression.

While for me it was a project of emotion from my heart, for Anubhav it was both his career, as well as on his stardom reputation.

Anubhav mentioned to me that expecting Paika Bidroh, he did not take up any Raja release films. Normally past 5 years he will always have a Raja and Dassera Festival release because the films bring in good revenue.

In those days Raja Release used to be extremely profitable as most people see a film during Raja

Holidays as a ritual. Good films made and released during Raja, reap good harvest of money. Top stars will always plan a Raja/Dassera release.

Being already in Aprll 2016 and Raja being hardly two months away, I asked Anubhav whether he can make a film in this short period of time and release it on Raja likely to fall around mid-June.

Anubhav was very enthusiastic and optimistic. He made a humble request that once I consent on the project he will take over of all responsibilities of implementing the project. In other words, he volunteered to be the line producer.

The only story he pursued with me was to remake a very successful Kanada film Ugram. The film's director Prashanta Neel went on to direct The KGF 1 and KGF2 later on. Ugram was a big hit in Kanada at that time.

My challenge was to localize the story suitable for Odisha and rather to do it better as it was my first venture of copy/paste culture that was killing Odisha Cineworld. I definitely liked the story, the Challenge of one character of hero turned villain, turned hero and end as a villain till climax. It was privilege that Mr Prashant Neel happily gave the film rights to take up this unpredictable challenge for me in Odisha.

On the date the film was announced renamed as "Agastya" which was the name of the hero in the film too, I openly told the press that I am doing a remake film but will endeavor to do it better than the original.

In the time of copy paste films in Odisha due to invasion of half trained South film personnel, my announcement of Agastya being remake of Kanada film and assurance that, I will try be make it better than the original earned quite a bit of appreciation with press and media for my candid confession. A reputed newspaper wrote that such gesture by Akshay Parija is truthful arrogance and Odisha expects such candidness from top rated filmmakers.

Agastya film making went on in breakneck speed. Anubhav gave his total commitment to complete the film on time though it was a herculean task.

Thanks to Odisha's well known music director Premanand, the music was an instant hit. The film gave first celluloid opportunity to little champ, young Ananya Sritam Nanda, who was Indian Idol Junior Season2 Champion.

As the film was in the Post Production stage, I learned for the first time that the theatrical halls are normally prebooked. Most of the halls in Odisha are already prebooked for two other films being planned to be released. One was by Tarang Group and the other one by earlier Sarthark owner, Mr Sitaram Agarwal. "Love Station" made by Tarang had Superstar

Babushan as hero and "Premare Premare" made by Sri Sitaram Agarwal had dashing Arindum as hero.

While both Tarang and Sitaram babu had about 50 halls prebooked by each of them, all that I was to get were only 12 halls but few top halls in important centers mostly due to the immense popularity of Anubhav being number one Star of Odisha.

Sitaram Babu who had sold his blood and sweat given channel Sarthak to Zee group, started communicating with me to work together and volunteered that he will postpone his film and all the halls will be given to Agastya.

Agastya being by Akshay Parija Production had already made waves. With Anubhav as hero, definitely it created ripples. The songs becoming super hits, added fire to the burning expectations of audience.

Coming to Odisha from Dubai, I met the Business Head of Zee Sarthak Mr Bhupesh Sharma on the Delhi / Bhubaneswar flight. He volunteered to sit next to me and by his ever-usual charming ways, he befriended me. He expressed a strong desire to acquire satellite rights of Agastya along with one more film of mine which was under production for the channel Zee Sarthak. As it is said, he made me an offer to buy the satellite rights at a price which I could not refuse.

Thus Agastya became the highest priced selling film for satellite ever paid to anyone at that time.

Though I was contacted by Tarang Channel to take satellite rights by matching the price, somehow I was not convinced as it was too late. Besides the bitter memory of the treatment by the elderly and respected CFO of Tarang during my earlier film was still fresh in my memory.

Agastya was released on June 12 with a lot of fanfare. Anubhav travelled in a decorated and branded open jeep with a large Band Party playing Agastya songs to Brindaban hall at Cuttack and the entire 2 KM road was jam packed with thousands of people. It was like a frenzy with over 10,000 people attending the premiere show. It was a nightmare even for me to enter the hall.

The film was a super hit from day one. While every actor and technicians did their work very well, the show stopper was Mr Akash Das Nayak for his dynamic work. A perceived victim in the story and getting back to his mighty, he instantly got into the hearts of audience with his powerful and measured acting. Such impact was there in his role that the audience left the halls after his dramatic penultimate scene thinking the film is over.

In the hurry of finishing the film, the producer's name was wrongly given, depriving me the pleasure of making the film. For a producer who spends all the money and possible profit or losses too, the name in prominence is the first reward which I was deprived very carelessly.

The film belongs to the hero where producer's hard earned money is invested, director and his team's hard work is invested. When the film becomes hit, normally it is the hero who gets the highest credit of Films. With lessor known star cast and if the film succeeds significantly the major credit goes to the Director.

The film Agastya being a super hit film, Anubhav's appreciation was significant. However, market spoke a lot about Akash Das Nayak and his last Scene.

Had Mr Sitaram Agarwal not betrayed in the last moment, the film could have been an all-time box office hit ever seen in Odisha. It grossed Rs 2.00 cores with only 12 halls. Had there been a 60 halls release, unless Mr Sitaram Agarwal's last minute change of mind, I could have been many times richer.

Yes, the mathematics was very right. But arithmetic was wrong.

The film came out better than the original Ugram. The songs were played out in marriage processions. Youngsters made video and posted in YouTube. The social media was evolving at that time. Had it been now, the songs could have broken many records.

However, whatever producer share that was to come did not come from halls and distributors and Rs 38.00 lacs remained unpaid. Whatever may be the excuse, nonpayment was wrong and illegal. I did not wish to go legal and assumed it as a loss like my earlier films.

Had I been guided on the importance of large number of hall releases, I could have postponed the film to Dassera just three months away and minted money. In money matters fate usually always plays a positive role for me, but this time it did not.

The mathematics being right was better than the arithmetic of unpleasant hall release and collection process.

● ● ●

THE MAKING OF PAIKA BIDROH

With many of my films not making money, though qualitatively considered excellent, or some decisions were foolish or immature, I was very much in a reverse gear.

I had never been worried about loss of money. I always trusted destiny.

However, my setback was the hard work put on by Manmohan Babu and my dream going waste for Paika Bidroh.

NMP, by that time a Padmshree Awardee and together we had created the famous film Kadvihawa in Hindi, had observed me from close quarters. He was very impressed with the project from day one. He knew the film will bring glory to Odisha, tell a lot about the untold stories of bravery, and faith to Lord Jagannath.

He proposed and I instantly agreed that I will make a docufilm on Paika Bidroh. My only objective was to tell the world the true story of Paika Bidroh and how crooked and cruel the Colonial rulers were.

British hanged Jai Rajguru in a brutal manner which breaks all war protocols in the world. Irrespective of war crimes, a country cannot humiliate or penalize the prisoners of war (PoW). Protocol stipulates that PoWs are to be treated humanely with dignity. In the wars in past the country of aggression is always made to compensate the losses either it was the first world war, or second or the last being Iraq war.

I always wished that someone after seeing the film, will file a multi-million-dollar legal suit in courts for the illegal brutality of the then Colonial rulers.

I wished to expose the Colonial British rulers. They first tried to insult Lord Jaganath, the most revered God of all Odiya's. Having failed to hit emotionally, they tried to hit under the belt by demonetization the prevailing coins and harvesting of Salt from Chilika, another livelihood of people. They could not succeed in this sinister design too.

When they decommissioned the Paika's from the Army on the pretext of non-familiarity with the latest weaponry, the Self Esteem of Paika's was affected. A Paika will be proud to be martyred in the war but can never sit down at home not fighting even if he is unwell. War cry brings in them lions strength and makes them forget any sickness, pain or Injury.

The last of their self-esteem was taken away with the decommissioning of Paikas from army. When I thought about the fate of the wives of Paika's and their children, tears would trickle. During the gorilla war, Paikas died in droves fighting in the forests. All dead were either eaten away by wild animals or their body got decomposed.

In Hindu tradition of death rituals, the dead-body must be cremated and the ashes has to be immersed in sacred waters at Puri Sea or Ganges river. The 12 day ritual will be performed at home by Brahmins and the sons.

If the body is not found and cremated, then the wife has to wait for 12 years as a married woman and will be a widow only after passing of 12 years. How painful and embarrassing it would have been for the lady who knows well that her husband will not came back but she has to pretend being married. How painful would have been for children waiting for their father who will never return.

Without going into the religious perceptions, I do realize that the soul remains on the earth in the absence of the death rituals. All those souls (Atrupta Atma) must be hovering on the earth with pain forever.

Over three large drinks in an evening, I emotionally expressed these fellings to NMP. He understood, he felt my pain and felt the genuineness of the Paika Bidroh project. Why it should not come to public knowledge which still have not been known nor have been told till date.

Next day morning he called me to his office and informed me that in the absence of the large money that was needed to make the film, we will make a docufilm to capture the emotional aspects that I narrated him the night before albeit in a sozzled state.

Though on a lesser scale, Paika Bidroh started to get a new life.

Sri Hara Prasad Das, retired Union Civil Servant and a famous poet, instantly agreed to write the script. He had one condition that there will be no caveat or disclaimer as is normal in a film. It says "the story is a work of fiction. Any resemblance is only coincidental".

Hara Babu insisted that his story will be purely based on elaborate research and if anybody objects and proves him wrong he is ready to face.

The production team was set up with NMP's longtime associate and experienced Anuj Tyagi leading the team and joining as a codirector. The making of the docufilm started.

The hands of an experienced Mumbai based Odiya maker Nischaya Rout was roped in. Madhav's wife Barnali Rath Panda joined me not only as Costume Director with her many Hindi film experiences, she also kindly agreed to be the coproducer to add to my loss of confidence.

Sarthak Anand, son of the legendary Odiya Actress Mrs Sujata Anand did the Production Manager role.

It was an emotional journey of the "dream coming true". National School of Drama products Manoj Mishra and Samaresh Routray had very kindly joined for the legendary characters of Jai Rajaguru and Buxi Jagabandhu.

The film required real technic of recreating the event 200 years back. The famous cinematographer Pratap Rout who did Agastya for me with highest competence and appreciation in Odiya cine world took the mantle of Director of Photography.

There definitely were multiple problems as happens in a film Production. Like sudden shortage of material, cost overruns etc. But the first cut was brilliantly and nicely worked out by Archit Rastogi, the eminent Editor from Mumbai.

The voice of a long-time associate, Durga Acharya added spice to the film and was appreciated by every reviewer who saw it. It was not about the quality of the film but the story that not many knew in Odisha.

As a surprise to me NMP handed me a packet of money with an amount of nearest to the cost supposed to be paid by unnamed well-wishers who were moved by the film and for bringing such a sensitive story to limelight. I still have a doubt that the money paid was a benevolence by him personally or some unknown well-wisher.

Paika Bidroha continued to be a hot topic with President of India Sri Pranab Mukherjee announcing it to be the First War of Independence. Both State and Central Government announced many measures to bring the Paika Bidroh to lime light.

The film went on to win Four State Film and Television Awards for the Best Telefilm, Best Direction, Best Cinematography and Best Editing. It was of immense satisfaction that in a single year I won the coveted The Best State Film Award (Mohan Suder Dev Goswami Award for Best Film) as well as the Best Telefilm Award.

Thanks to NMP for his consistent advice, guidance and creative supervision for which a rare document any film for next hundred years was created.

I could not have been happier for being both arithmetically right and significantly right mathematically too.

● ● ●

THE BENGAL JOURNEY: TO THE LAND OF CREATIVITY

The Emirates direct nonstop flight from Dubai to Los Angles(LA) takes almost 16 hours. It leaves Dubai early in the morning and reaches by about late noon. With the body clock day time, flight path in day time, spending time inside a flight for such long hours is highly uncomfortable irrespective of the shutters down and night like ambience on the flight.

I was travelling to Los Angeles to attend Indian International Film Festival where Kadvihawa was selected in the feature film category. It was an honour with the selection of the film in the festival at the heart of film world Hollywood. Though I had travelled to

Los Angeles on business on many occasions, being there in Hollywood and that too as an invitee of a film that has been selected in the festival was both an honor and pleasure.

The excitement was natural with the hope of getting to meet few film personalities around the globe. I also had an appointment with a Hollywood based curator who could guide on the Oscar formalities. As a filmmaker, it obviously is always a dream to be in a Oscar list someday. I definitely had the dream to be at least India's nomination to Oscar for Kadvihawa, probably the first feature film dealing with Global Warming and Climatic Change as early as in 2016.

My normal travel routine to United States is always to take Emirates because of its direct connections from Dubai besides, of course, the Emirates hospitality is world famous. The Airbus A380 service that flies to Los Angeles with its upper deck sky cabin was and probably still is, the best first class travel experience in the world.

The Sky Bar in Upper Deck of Airbus A380 is an experience always to remember.

A full-fledged bar with the choicest of drinks of rare single malts, wine selections, warmly made cocktails by the ever attentive air hostesses and the wide range of hors d'oeuvres makes it a dreamy feeling of a bar 40,000 feet above the sea level in the sky. It is also a great place to interact with many personalities from around the world.

Sometimes, I use a mild anti-anxiety pill to kill the long hours of travel. It is neither a medically approved process and probably illegal too. I would take a pill before boarding. The extraordinary service that is offered in the first class would have to wait. I would have a glass or two of Dom Perignon Champagne, some Beluga Caviar and a croissant. The special full bed Sky Cabins will be neatly laid once the seat belt signs are off. The anti-anxiety tablet would make me sleep for almost 8 to 10 hours nonstop. It would not be deep sleep but relaxed sleep.

I would get up very refreshed. Emirates Airbus A380 provides a shower room at 40,000 feet and that's an experience to cherish. I would take a shower not just to feel fresh but for the experience of taking bath at 40,000 feet in air. I am, of course the same person who had travelled happily in a 30 seater bus with over 120 Passengers shoved inside the bus besides cattle and chickens with the distance from my village to Cuttack 50 km away taking more than 8 hours.

It is said not to fly high but remain grounded to the roots. I do remain grounded to my humble roots. Never the less the experiences make me happy.

After shower, I would have few vodka martini and have carefully prepared launch followed by few glasses of exotic selected wines. Starting in the early morning hours from Dubai, the flight lands at Los Angles at 1.30 p.m. in their afternoon. It gives an interesting feeling of 6 hours travel in spite of the 16-hour travel due to time zone changes. Anti-anxiety pill followed by 10-hour sleep does not create the Jet lag which is very common for travel between Asian subcontinent and American continent.

On the day of travel to Los Angles, to attend the Indian Intentional Film Festival at LA 2017, I realized at Dubai airport, that too after the check in and security process was over that I had forgotten to carry the anti-anxiety pill in the hand bag. My routine of the pill was neither an addiction nor a must for my travels. I take it rarely only when I am travelling long distance flights to West and was quite tired at work. I strongly advice readers not try this experiment which probably suited me but may be dangerous to others!!

In Emirates there are many ways to kill the time to relax on a long haul flight. More than one thousand films in over two dozen languages and the best of selections of films from around the world are there to select. It also has many regional film sections from India. Of course, the great Emirates hospitality with breakfast, lunch, dinner and abundance of alcoholic and non-alcoholic beverages flowing, passing time is comfortable. The best they do is to serve food every six hours but may be called launch or dinner depending on time of the zone its flying.

As the plane was about to take off, I opted for some selected Single Malts and a full breakfast platter along with glasses of red wine. It is customary for the receptive and efficient hostesses to always take orders before take-off to ask what the traveler will opt for after take-off and seat belt signs are off.

I still have the bad habit of falling asleep after breakfast. I slept but hardly for two hours.

When I started planning how to spend next 14 hours, I was worried as I did not carry any book to read too. So the only option was to watch films. Emirates sky cabins are fitted with excellent LED Screens. Viewing is as good as home viewing on a large TV.

I found most of the Hindi films I had already seen. I normally do not see English Films in flight because I still cannot understand English films fluently without Subtitles.

Few more hard drinks followed by a good lunch of grilled fish and sleep again took away almost 14 hours.

The last two hours is normally uncomfortable. It is natural due to the long hours of being inside a controlled pressure cabin.

I was no exception. I walked to the sky bar in Airbus A380 for two reasons; just a bit of walk and forget the anxiety with few more drinks or chatting with a other passengers.

I did not find many passengers at the bar. I ordered a single malt and tried to attract the air hostess for a chat. She was not welcoming with all the demands of hard work with long hours. I came back to my sky cabin and started scanning the films on the TV screen. Just a thought came to me to see any regional movie to kill the last two hours. I scanned Malayalam, Tamil, Telugu and Punjabi Films but nothing attracted me. Then came Bengali films under the regional films category.

I had not seen more than two or three Bengali films in my life till that time. Other than the greats like Satyajit Ray, Mrinal Sen, Ritwik Ghatak, Buddhadeb Dasgupta, Tapan Sinha and Gautam Ghosh, I was also aware of the superstars of Bengali films like Uttam Kumar, Saumitra Chatterjee and Prasanjit. I also was aware of a name Ritupurna Sengupta, a beauty from Bengali cinema. I immensely liked her in a Hindi film "Main, Meri Patni Aurr Woh". The film was about a short height man marrying a tall and beautiful wife.

I saw the name of Prasanjit and Ritupurna Sengupta in a film and instantly played it.

The film was such that it attracted me within the first few minutes to continue watching. I was glued to the film with its extremely engaging and emotional story. With the sensitive acting by many top stars, it had made the film extra attractive.

Interfering with film which pauses automatically, the pilot announced approaching the landing at Los Angles. Luckily in Emirates first class the TV continues working. I continued watching till the flight landed and with announcement of deplaning.

The film was on a very critical, sensitive and at a tricky stage. It was painful for me to stop watching and leave the film without completing to know the end.

I had two options either to sit down and continue watching till the end. In that case in immigration, I could be behind five hundred passengers that an Airbus A380 carries. Ideally, as a first class passenger, I would be first or second person in immigration and would go out in few minutes.

I carried the film in my mind with lot of confusion as to what is going to be the end of the story. The film, a romantic story line of separation of husband and wife and many conclusions that came to my mind as to what will be the end.

I carried the film in my mind and whenever the thought came, I will be visualizing of some end to the film either a happy ending or sad ending.

The film was where Prasanjit is separated from his beautiful wife Rituparna due to maladjustment in life. She is coming back to Kolkota from Mumbai, metamorphic indication that probably she is going back to reconcile with her estranged husband. She is disgusted in her first class coupe with an uncouth, unpolished talkative woman with a child. And as the woman's much awaited husband joins her, it was found to be Prasanjit thus demolishing her hopes.

And that's where I had to Switch of the TV on the flight.

My imagination was going wild what would have happened? How the director will end the film? I was neither knowing or was aware of the name of the director at that time.

I thought may be the other woman was sympathetically given shelter by the hero for some unfortunate reason and all will be well on his wife's return.

The other woman will be settled in her household and it will be happy ending.

Next three days I remained engaged in the festival, press interviews, parties and few meetings.

Kadvihawa did not make to any award on the final round. The festival was agog with a young phenomenon, Ms Reema Das whose 'Village Rockstar' had won the National Award for the Best Film that year. The same film also won the Best Film in the Festival.

On my return flight from Los Angeles to Dubai, after settling down on my seat in sky cabin, 1 A in Emirates Airbus A380, first class, first thing I did was to open the TV and go to the film. The hostesses were probably a bit annoyed with my lack of attention to their cold towel and other typical Airbus A380 formalities of overnight toilet bag and gift bag of Emirates.

I was in shock with myself. Contrary to my various predictions, the end was unusual but that's how it had to end. It was significantly logical, natural and probably the best end.

Being a well-known and emotional personality, I was shattered with the end but in creativity I could not get any other option than what was the end of the film.

After three Blue label scotches, I was still thinking. I rewinded the film to see the name of the director.

And it was not one but a duo of Mrs Nandita Ray and Mr Siboprosad Mukherjee.

As I was not conversant with Bengali Cinema, I did not have any idea about them.

I scanned the regional Bengali Section again for some other Bengali film of the same director duo and found a film named Belasheshe.

Obviously, I started seeing the movie Belasheshe also. I was in high spirit, or the spirit of the film was high, I did not know how the time passed, but I watched it nonstop till end and was spellbound.

My usual feeling of being high with alcohol was gone and I was as cool as waking up in morning. I was still thinking about the film Belasheshe that I just saw.

I was at a loss to think how one can perceive a story line like Belasheshe. Extremely unusual but absolutely logical with the end having million-dollar messages. The message was so beautiful that I was absolutely thunder struck again.

The flight that time must be cruising over Canada airspace to Greenland and down to Europe and Middle East as per the flight path shown on the screen.

The Emirates on board clock was showing the time zone in India was early morning. I made an on air call to a friend Mr Biraja Prasad Kar, a Cinematographer and Professor at Satyajit Ray Film and Television Institute at Kolkata. He had worked as DOP in one of my films 'Bye Bye Dubai' shot in Odisha and Dubai too. I did not wish to wait till I land in Dubai after about 13 hours more. The on air roaming facility was also available on

Emirates all thru the route auto transferring to various countries as it flies over.

He must have been surprised by a funny number of the call from over the North pole. He was surprised with my call too. I requested him that he must use all his power and influence and fix me an appointment with the director duo of Mrs Nandita Ray and Mr Siboprosad Mukherjee after three days. The desire was to meet such creative personalities and learn from their experiences. After reaching Dubai, the next day I got a message from Sri Biraja Kar that a meeting is arranged with Mr Mukherjee the day after, at 3 pm.

The Emirates Dubai-Kolkata flight was at an odd hour of 1.30AM midnight that lands at about 8.30 am morning. As I assumed a minimum of 45 minutes meeting with Mr. Siboprosad Mukharjee, fixed at 3PM afternoon, I booked my return flight straight from Kolkata to Dubai Sunday Evening at 8.30 PM

I had checked in to the Swissotel Hotel near the airport which is now changed to Taj City Centre.

Myself and Mr. Kar went to the office of Mr. Mukherjee to be on time for the 3 PM meeting.

The office was very typical of a Kolkata Bengali culture office located at the busy Ballygunj area sub lanes which in spite of the Google GPRS system was very difficult to locate.

Though we started with sufficient time on hand, still we got a bit delayed, confused with the location.

Mr. Mukherjee was warm in welcoming us speculating about my intention of visit, I had not given any reason for the meeting other than courtesy call.

Mr. Mukherjee must have Googled my name and found me to be a regional film producer with multiple National and State Film Awards but nothing to really boast about.

He was warm to receive me and the great Bengali hospitality was evident with offers of lunch, snacks, sweets and of course tea.

I could not avoid the attraction of the typical Bengali samosa and red tea.

My first question to Mr Mukherjee was "what is the intoxicant he uses"? He appeared extremely surprised and embarrassed. I clarified again that what recreational substance he uses like alcohol, marijuana, opium or any other drugs!!

He appeared very uncomfortable, edgy and on the verge of irritation. Instead of putting me off, he was polite to express what sort of a question was this and why do I ask such question? May be seeing my age at plus side of sixty he was decent and polite.

"How do you perceive such unusual and exceptional story line like Praktan and Belasheshe??

These extraordinary ideas sometimes come only with the genius mind or from a person travelling in another world with the influence of special stimulants!!" I spoke nonstop and looked at him with worry that I probably rubbed him on wrong side taking such liberty with someone considered a celebrity.

He smiled with the muscles on his face relaxing. He first touched the photograph kept on his table which he explained as his beloved mother. Then he raised his hand above and directed to God. "These two are my mediums of intoxication. Their blessings have infused the ideas in me. Whatever I am, whatever I create are all because of their blessings".

He was so calm and genuine in his expression that even if I would have been blind, I would have believed.

The very brief interaction probably was an exchange of unlimited mutual trust and faith in both of us towards each other.

Mr. Kar left after 15 minutes and without realizing the time and my return flight, the 20 minutes meeting ended up being three-hour interaction.

The three hours was as if I was reading a biography of Shiboprosad. He took me thru his struggle to the present spanning over a decade.

I am a known introvert and do not interact with people I do not know closely. But I probably have a God given personality, wherein, many a genuine people feel very emotionally confident and confide in me themselves. May be because I am a good listener too.

It was only at 6 PM that I realized I have a flight to catch at 8.30 pm that night and that too an international flight for which one has to reach at least two hours before departure due to many of the travel formalities.

In his talk, Mr. Mukherjee was narrating about his commitments and convictions to make a film that must touch the emotional cord of the audience. You have to give them an emotional connection. They need to find themselves in it.

This one example was classic for me. He explained that when we watch a film we know in two and half hours it will end, either happily or sadly. But we get edgy and angry on the villain, get emotional with the sufferings of the protagonist forgetting that it is just a film.

A good film must make the audience forget their existence for those few hours. They must swim or sink with the flow of the film uncertain of the end irrespective of the fact that there will be an end to the film.

A director who could enable such journey of an audience is a people's director and he always aspires to be one.

"I work for entertainment. I work for box office not for awards". He was as candid as possible.

He was very apologetic that I am going to miss my flight. I ordered one more round of Samosa to make him feel relaxed. Instead, he suggested the very typical Bengali evening snack of 'Mudhi with Channa fry' followed by aromatic red tea. Later I realized no evening is complete without the 'Mudhi', the putted rice and sew or channa or pakoda etc in the Bengali house or office in an evening. Eating these snacks together symbolizes a bonding.

Unknowingly or unintentionally I got bonded with Mr. Shiboprosad Mukherjee that afternoon which stretched over into the evening.

It was towards the end of our long lively meeting that he informed me of his new venture, a sequel to Belasheshe. It will be named as Belashuru. I was at a loss to think of a story beyond the most appropriate end of Belasheshe. Mr Mukherjee in his most charming way explained that Belashure will be more sensitive with the same protagonists of revered Shri Soumitra Chatarjee and Ms Swatilekha Sengupta. Relationships will be reflected in a different trajectory.

Having seen Belasheshe and fully charmed by its unusual but interesting content, I already had a lot of confidence on the creative capacity of the duo of Shiboprosad and Nandita Ray. I instantly volunteered to be a part of Belashuru if the option is available. Mr. Mukherjee was delighted with my instant offer and promised to revert back at the earliest.

My return to Swissotel took me almost one hour and 15 minutes in the busy evening traffic of Kolkata. But the reflections of the time spent and the positive vibration created gave me an unusual happiness.

I changed the ticket to next day morning flight.

After refreshment in the room, I hit the bar and few quick Chivas cooled my excitement.

After almost 22 years, I was spending a night in Kolkata in July 2018. Kolkata had significantly changed.

I decided to become young again of the mid-twenties when Kolkata was a dream destination with its glittering night life and mouthwatering food. But unfortunately the area of newly developed Kolkata was far from the exciting Kolkata of seventies. I ended up with some not so great Bengali food in the restaurant of the hotel.

I hit the bed early for the early morning flight not so happy for the dull Kolkata night experience. But some internal positivity of something good is destined, induced good sleep that night.

Almost two months passed after I met Mr. Mukherjee. Though creatively he remained a much taller figure, we addressed each other as 'Sir'. There were few WhatsApp interactions, when I saw two other films of 'Posto' and 'Hami' in Hoichoi OTT made by the duo. Windows Production house was created by Ms Nandita Ray and Mr. Shiboprosad Mukherjee. A veteran in media and creativity, Ms Nandita Ray was already a cult figure in both large and small screen. Shiboprosad Mukherjee, another veteran in both small as well as large screen joined hands with Ms Ray and Windows was born. As is said one plus one makes eleven. The duo of Shibo and Nandita made debut with their directional venture 'Ichhe' in 2011. Together they had churned out 10 films in 7 years. They became known for making socially relevant films which are also entertaining to viewers. By the time we met, they already made popular new age films like Praktan, Belasheshe, Muktadhara, Ramdhenu, Posto and Hami, most of which are moderate to big box office success.

While watching Posto and Hami, Shiboo and myself had long interactions over Phone discussing the good and bad part of the films. My minute observation of many scenes and the questions on origination of the ideas was appreciated by him. What I immensely liked in him was the dedication of each appreciation to his mother and God. He never boasted or took credit for any exceptional work. Besides his mother and God, he also always gave great credit to Nandita didi, as he called her.

I was sold to Shiboo's humbleness and team leadership. In my career of film making till I met Shiboo, most of the directors I worked with were mini narcissists who took all credit for good work and blamed others for failures.

By mid-September Mr. Shiboprosad called and inquired if I am likely to be in Mumbai by last week as he is expected to visit Mumbai for about 10 days and proposed to meet to discuss further on the prospects of working together for the Belashuru project.

I was about to sign on a new fiction show with Zee Sarthak in Odisha and scheduled to come, hence I routed my travel to Odisha via Mumbai.

I reached Mumbai in late evening and was scheduled to meet Mr Shiboprosad next day morning over breakfast in his hotel.

Both of us are early risers. Many a times we interact early in the mornings. We met at the scheduled time of 8.30 am at the hotel breakfast lobby. Though it was our second meeting but there already existed quite a bit of familiarity. He requested to move to the open lounge overlooking the Arabian sea which was less crowded. I rather liked the view of the sea and shifted there.

Mr Shiboprosad took out a note pad and pen and started writing something to my inquisitive eyes.

He listed 6 films named as Manoj da'r Adbhut Bari, Rasagolla, Mukharji Da' ra Bou, Kontho, Gotro and Belashuru. Out of these 6 films, two are in final stages of completion, the third Kontho is at 60% completion. The other three are at pre-production stage.

He further explained that the first three are directed by three other promising directors but under full supervision of Windows. The last three are under direct direction of the due Nandita Ray and Shibo Prosad Mukherjee.

I was feeling a bit awkward why Mr Mukherjee was showing such minute business details of his company. He probably read my face and clarified. He said from the day we met he found me to be very passionate about films and not look into the mathematics of films. But he is concerned for both mathematics and passion. Hence he is talking to me with such confidence.

Then he ignited the bomb in front of me "If you are willing to participate in real quality films, please join Windows as a Partner for all the six films". Said Mr. Mukharjee adding that it's a rare opportunity he is offering me for just being convinced of my personality as well as ambition to do good films".

Here I am placed on peak of a mountain straight from where I can see only sunshine and nothing else. Falling from the peak of the mountain could be end of my life.

I was unable to even think further. Bengali cinema and market for cinema is not very well known to me. I know in Odisha it used to take me a year from concept to completion of a film. Here I am being offered to do Six films in two years. The major hassle of distribution and collection, an unfortunate corrupt and crooked activity in Odisha, will also be handled by Windows.

As I remained blank in my mind and unable to even eat my breakfast, Mr. Mukherjee took out another paper from his bag and placed before me. It was like from nowhere a white rat being taken out under the magic hat. He had signed a deal with Star Jalsa for a composite figure of Rs. 7.00 Crores for these films. It is only for satellite Rights. The Musical and Digital rights will still remain with the producer. The figure was almost 80% of the cost of making. The theatrical collection from Box office is bonus.

All I could calculate is that 80% of investment is already secured. The 20% can be definitely covered through digital and music rights. Even if the film does not work, my money is safe.

I expressed my deepest thanks and gratitude for taking me into confidence. I expressed my 'in principle' agreement to plunge into the opportunity further. I promised to come to Kolkata after his return and take things forward.

Least I know or ethically not shared by Mr Mukherjee that he was the Jury for the selection of India's entry into OSCAR that year. Kadwihawa, the dream Project of me and NMP was also competing for the nomination that year.

As per schedule I flew to Odisha that afternoon and straight drove to Zee Sarthak office.

Mr Rahul Rao, Chief Channel Officer of Zee Sarthak who had exclusive experience in Bengal Market. I assumed he will be the best person for guidance.

He obviously was very conversant about Windows and the duo of Shiboprosad and Nandita Ray. He was quite optimistic on them and was confident about their creative capabilities.

When I gave the list of 6 films that I propose to get associated, he was a bit conservative in his impression about the three films directed by other than the duo. However, he made a professional statement that if given a choice, I should blindly accept the three films to be directed by Nandita Ray and Shiboprosad. He had his doubts on box office potential of the film not directed by the Duo.

There was nobody else I could ask for advice! People who were assumed to be my genuine well-wishers and proactive advisers were never the same in their heart. They preferred to say what I will like and enjoyed my financial failures.

I did not know anybody in Kolkata to seek advice. Normal acquaintances were in appreciation of the films made by Nandita & Shiboo.

My banker's instinct came in to play with 80% of investment already secured, contrary to the full risk I had experienced in most of my films in Odiya and Hindi, I decided to take the plunge.

I was in Windows office at Kolkata after Mr Mukharjee's return from the Oscar review meet.

The day, which I cannot remember now, was very auspicious. Mr. Mukherjee, a very decisive person as I found him, opined to seal the agreement same day.

He brought his friend, lawyer, counsellor and whose number he has saved as "God" Mr Soumyadip for the meeting and advice on the draft of the agreement.

I did not like Mr. Soumyadip as I always see Lawyers and Police with apprehension. However, I definitely appreciated his legal acumen and expertise. Obviously as Legal Adviser to Windows, the interest of Windows is paramount to him.

He prepared a brief draft where in the business plan was as under.

1. I will invest full in the film for the Production.

2. Windows will put all their efforts and expertise to make a good film.
3. Windows will organize sponsored marketing cost.
4. Actual cost of marketing will be spent by Windows.
5. After release of the film, the marketing cost will get paid first from the net theatrical collections.

6. After I, as full investor, recover the investment fully, the profits will be shared 50:50 between us.
7. Satellite and digital income will be shared in higher side to Windows and lower side to me.

During most of our conversation with Shiboo, he did share strongly that most of his recent past films were box office success. I had also heard by that time his recent past two films, Posto and Hami did exceptionally well. Hence one can hope at least 100% recovery of the investment. Anything over it is a bonus for me. With my cinema experience in Odiya and Hindi, even recovery of money continued to be a distant dream.

Loss in investment, including holding cost for a year, with my normal rules of investment was failing. I comforted myself that the loss of expected return is compensated with my entry into Bengali cinema and working with the best of Directors.

I agreed to the terms and we signed a stamp paper Agreement to join together for the next 6 films on that day.

When press grilled me for my investment shift from Odisha to Bengal I replied honestly that 'I had gone there not to earn but to learn'.

First film "Manoj da'r Adbhut Bari" was released in Dashera 2018. It was not directed by the duo of Shiboo and Nandita jee. As conveyed by Shiboo, the film did well. I never asked for either the accounts or the theatrical collection. I always believed that if you trust someone, then trust fully. If the trust has failed it was bad luck. Somehow, I had not been very fortunate with people I trusted. It could go 70% to trust betrayed.

The next film Rasagolla was released in December 2018. I was very excited to attend the premier of the film. I was made to address the packed audience in the hall. Unfortunately, I had to speak in English as I cannot speak in Bengali, though I can fully understand and can read too. It was an extremely happy occasion to attend the premiere. I met the glitterati of Bengali Cinema there.

Rasgolla was an Iconic Film depicting the creation of the sweet dish by the famous Bengali confectioner of Kolkata in early 20th century. The film became a controversy in Odisha as Bengal and Odisha were fighting over who invented Rasgolla. Bengal had taken the GI registration already and Odisha was fuming. I unfortunately got a back lash back home for being an Odia and making a film in Bengali about Rasgolla. However, after seeing the film which didn't depict Rasgolla being invented in Bengal, the rough feathers of lovers of Rasgolla in Odisha were soothed.

Next two films were getting completed and released in Feb 2019 and May 2019.

The first film "Mukharjee Dar Bou", though made on a lower budget by a newcomer lady director Ms Pritha Chakroverty, it was an instant success.

The next film 'Kantho', was a cinematic marvel and till date my most valuable film in my evolution of making 33 films till date. Ms Nandita Ray was the Writer Director along will Shiboo. The film was a phenomenal success. While Shiboo himself acted as Protagonist cancer patient, the two lady characters of Paoli Dams and the Bangladesh's phenomenal sensation Joya Ahsan were spectacular. The film broke many box office records. It was also shortlisted for the India's nomination to Oscar 2018.

In the meanwhile, the 5th film Gotro (Clan) had started. We had planned to shoot a part of the film in Odisha to take advantage of the new film policy announced by the Hon Chief Minister of Odisha Shri Naveen Patnaik in March 2019. As per the policy, non Odiya films shot in Odisha are promised significant subsidies.

The film had a rare shoot at Bukhari Pir Saheb, Kaipadar, Khurda. The local management of the Mosque were very hesitant to allow shooting around the sacred mosque.

A place of pride in India on religious harmony, the place is amalgamation of Muslim Mystics and the Hindu Religion.

They were apprehensive of the face that earlier shoots by few films and probably not with right respect, there were few causalities in the area, which they felt was a curse. After I explained my three decades of living in the Islam world of Middle East and with immense respect to the religious faiths, they agreed.

The Directors wished to redo the most famous folk song of Odisha i.e. Rangabati, a phenomenon for over 60 years and include it in the film. I tried to get the rights but since there were no rights holder I could connect; I gave newspaper advertisement. No one made any claim to the rights.

The song was redone in Bengali by Mr Surojit Chatterjee and Ms Iman Chakraborty. The song became a phenomenon instantly and broke all viewing records over the songs created by others. The song mentioned the names of the composer Mr Prbhudatta Prdhan and the Lyricist Mr Mitrabhanu Gauntia. I started getting calls from Odiyas around the world recognizing that thru the song they could know about other contributors than the singers Jitendra Haripl and Krishna Patel. Mr Haripal was conferred Padmashree in 2017. Post the phenomenal success of the song and spread over the world, the Lyricist Mr Mitrabhnu Gauntia was conferred Padmashree and later on in 2023, the female singer Mrs Krishna Patel was also conferred Padmashree. Mr Prabhudatta Pradhan, the composer unfortunately was no more to get the honor.

The film Gotro dealt with the religious harmony in our work(karma) than on the basis of our birth.

Gotro became one more film after Kontho that I felt immensely satisfied and proud of.

I hope the Director duo will carve out Gotro 2 in near future.

My tryst with Windows, Shiboprosad and Nandita Didi continues till date and the arithmetic calculations of the relationship is still premature.

In simple words we say "chapal ghis gaya". I have made dozens of visits to Windows. Talked on many projects.

But nothing materialized as yet in last five years. My financial negativity could not satisfy Shiboo's 'bring money, will work and make money."

However, the Mathematics has been greatly positive till date and I am sure will continue to swell in coming days, months and years, thus making my association arithmetically positive too.

● ● ●

(Kuwait Tower)

DREAMS, UNCERTAINTY AND UNKNOWN JOURNEY

When I told my mother in February 1983, that I got a job in Kuwait with ten times salary of what I was getting in India as a Bank officer, her face became pale. Contrary to my expectations that she will be very happy for my rare achievement in those days to get a direct management cadre job in an International Bank overseas, she was very silent.

xxxxxxxxxxx

Getting the promotion to a management cadre in those days in mid-seventies, from a clerical position within three and half years, can be considered very early and an achievement too. The day I finished my graduation exam, I had no intention to pursue Post Graduation. Instead I joined as Cashier with Indian Overseas Bank. The early promotion was possible due to my completion of post-graduation while working besides completing the much difficult CAIIB Exam, a must for all bankers those days, either to get promotion from clerical cadre to officer cadre or to various higher grades in officer's cadre. I had joined as a cashier three and half years back and got promoted in the earliest time thru a process of internal written test and interview.

My first posting was at Lucknow as there were not many places with more than one branch. My wife being a direct recruit Probationary Officer and having already completed her probation, it was assumed that she will be posted in same town as me but in different branches.

Lucknow was a beautiful city as I first saw people with natural love for flowers. Extremely cultured in their language, behavior, and of extremely generous nature, I fell in love with Lucknow on my first arrival. The cycle rickshaw I was travelling from station to hotel on my arrival had a narrow escape on road. Contrary to Odisha where the rickshaw puller would shout with vulgar language, he just said "why you wish to commit suicide brother". I realized Lucknow is a place of great culture.

Lucknow continues to be one of my most cherished experiences despite my short tenure. Being out of the home place and to restart a life of my own, definitely I had initial setbacks of settling down due to lack of enough resources besides challenges.

xxxxxxxxxx

Two years of stay in Lucknow was very satisfying both professionally and personally. I was recognized as a good worker and at the same time family life was quite good with developing of friendship with many people both locals as well as from Odisha.

Money continued to be a challenge due to various commitments and unplanned expenses in in the past.

However, my dreams and ambitions were always high, to grow in life and succeed much better than expected. I was aware that a career in banking is going to be thru the normal process of time bound promotions. Even if one excels in the job, promotion comes once in seven years. For next grade, another five years to a senior grade.

In my early Odisha days, one of my friend's younger brother, a ceramic technologist, had got a job in Kuwait. I was quite fascinated observing his extra money earning capacity and use of foreign made clothing as well as other foreign gadgets. In those days in early eighties, in a backward India, products of foreign origin was a dream.

I continued to look at the possibilities of an International Bank job, which were very few in India those days.

One morning, while reading the newspaper, a habit to read it first thing in morning, I came across an advertisement for position in an International Bank and the requirement was five years of work experience.

As per total banking experience, I had almost qualified but mine was a mix of clerical as well as officer's experience. Nevertheless, I applied. It was self-typed on an old Remington typewriter and there are many mistakes in the application. However, it was brief but expressive of my education and experience. I conveyed about the advertisement to everyone in the bank and about 8 people also applied. All of them had better education and experience than me. All of us forgot about the application. Months flew by with a busy professional life.

I was dedicated to my job and worked hard. I worked late hours till about 7.30 pm against the 5 pm bank closing hours. It was one of those evenings where in, myself as well as most my senior colleagues were present till late hours. The postman came inside the bank and delivered a telegram to the Branch Manager. In those days, quicker mode of communications used to be either telegram or telex or trunk calls only. The telegram was addressed to me. But the Branch Manager could not in any manner decipher it. He brought it to me and handed over commenting it to be some kind of fraud as the telegram read:

"Myself and Mr Tawfiq, Chief Executive Officer will be present for an interview for you at Hotel Taj Intercontinental, Bombay (now Mumbai). Kindly be present on 15th July 1982 with all documents. Best regards. Ahmed Al Hilal, Executive Manager, Administration. Burgan Bank, Kuwait"

For me also it appeared some French language until I remembered that I made an application for a position in an International Bank thru a post box number only. Excitedly I inquired with other colleagues if anyone else got the telegram. It was negative from all. Moreover, most thought it to be a hoax. My personal feeling was it to be genuine, and I must attempt it. I drove back home in the Bullet I had those days, probably a bit faster speed out of excitement to consult my wife, who instantly suggested I must attempt.

Observing that we were on 12th July night and in Lucknow which is very much away from trunk routes of Delhi/Calcutta /Madras to Bombay, only way to reach Bombay was to catch a train next morning that leaves at about 10 am from Lucknow Central and reaches Bombay VT by next day evening after 32 hours.

Then came the problem of money. By mid-month all salary used to get exhausted. My wife revealed that she still holds the Rs 600 house rent to be given to the land lord but was not given as he was out of town. We decided to take the risk of default that month and I planned out the travel next day morning using that money.

In Odisha, as it is not a cold place, we rarely stitch suits unlike in north India. I only had an off white suit that I stitched for my marriage reception. I packed the suit and few other accessories in a suitcase and started the journey next day morning towards an uncertainty. It was my official visit to Bombay, the other one was years back as a tourist.

The highly overcrowded train, being only train in a day, was unfortunately overbooked and my persuasion with the Ticket Checkers on the spot was fruitless. With no options available, I forced myself into the general compartment with the suitcase on my head. The Suitcase was a VIP luggage those days unlike the versatile luggage carriers available now. I was carrying it on my head because there was absolutely

absolutely no place in the compartment for the suitcase to keep. The train started and I was standing inside the train with the suitcase on my head. It was so jam packed that I would not fall out of balance with the movement of train, nor I was even required to hold on to the rouling for support.

An hour later, after reaching Kanpur I could place the suitcase on the upper luggage deck and was much comfortable to continue standing. The whole day and the whole night passed standing. Being an express train it had less stops. However, I cannot go out as I will lose my standing place. The night passed too standing in the compartment. By early morning the train stopped at a station called Bhusawal in Maharashtra. I realized that the train has crossed UP and Madhya Pradesh as well. Surprisingly many passengers got down there. And I could get a seat for myself. I was almost fainting with hunger but was worried to go out lest I lose my suitcase. The station was full of banana stalls on carts. I picked up few bananas and savored it with the satisfaction as if I am having a full thali meal.

The train started for Mumbai. The stress and strain made me half asleep. By noon, I found a young smart man and we picked up a conversation. He was a sailor in Commercial Shipping and was on home vacation but was travelling back on an urgent call of duty. When he heard my story of the nightmarish travel he was sympathetic. He suggested me a hotel that are mostly frequented by Sailors and price was Rs 60 per day against a normal price of Rs 300 per day of Hotels in Nariman Point and the Port area. We communicated many a thing. Mostly I learned all about shipping and the operations. He was the sailor in a Dry Bulk Carrier ferrying iron Ores from Goa to China those days.

The train reached Mumbai and we warmly bid good byes to each other, he wishing me good luck for my interview and I wishing him good luck for his sailing. Unlike present days where we exchange phone numbers or instantly get connected thru social media, we never had that practices at that time in 1982 and we never got connected. Twenty-Eight years later I became a Cofounder and Executive Director of a large Shipping Company owning many Oil carriers and Dry Bulk Carriers I fondly remembered the gentleman.

I checked into the hotel suggested by him which I found was quite good besides being inexpensive. As suggested by him the food was excellent with value for money in the restaurant of the hotel. My anxiety of the genuineness of the interview and the process of interview were weighing heavy on my mind. My sleep was not as deep despite the hectic train travel.

Next day morning I inquired about the location of Taj Intercontinental Hotel which was hardly ten minutes away. I started at 8.45 am all suited and booted for the so called interview and the uncertainties.

Contrary to my apprehension, there was a board in the hotel lobby guiding interviewees to a suite in the old Taj wing. In my life, it was my first ever step into a Five Star Hotel. All that I had ever experienced was standing in front of both Oberoi and Taj Hotels at Nariman Points and observing the glitter of cars and big people.

I reached the large suite and was warmly welcomed by an Indian gentleman. I found there were about twenty other candidates who had already reached. While talking, it was told that about 30 candidates will be interviewed that day on 15_{th}. The process is supposed to be going on for last two days and that day on 15_{th} was the last day.

The gentleman who received me and others introduced himself as Dr Menezes and informed that the process will start at about 9.30 am. My turn probably came at about 11 am and I was guided to another spacious suite next door.

I greeted the gentlemen in the suite warmly, a typical Lucknow style of humbleness that I have learned in Lucknow. As being said, a Lucknowite will win the hearts of even enemies instantly by his "Aadab".

May be my young age, fit and slim body and the mild colored well fitted suit created a bit of instant positiveness. I was made to sit comfortably and offered tea or coffee, which I politely declined out of tension. A barrage of academic questions started from both the gentlemen. It was related to mostly banking and few were on legal matters. I got a feeling that the first question's crisp and correct answer by me encouraged them for the next question and finding prompt answers, they were feeling encouraged to ask more and more questions. I would owe my answers for my hard work on the CAIIB Banking Examination that I had passed. I also got happy and thankful to God to be asked more questions as more and more questions give always an opportunity to prove oneself better. I knew, I was answering correctly and could realize happiness from the body language of the interviewers.

After almost forty minutes of questions and my answers, it was some light moment as one gentleman asked the other if he has still more questions. The small smile with "no more questions" surely gave me some comfort and optimism.

They just inquired if I have any relatives in Middle East and how enthusiastic I am to work in Middle

East. I neither have any relatives and obviously and enthusiastically consented for working in Middle East. Ending the conversation warmly they handed me a piece of paper and told me to contact Dr Menezes. The paper had rules and regulations of Kuwait printed. I did not find anything of substance in the paper.

I was confused to know the fate of interview and went to Dr Menezes. He inquired whether I was given any paper. When I showed the paper, he just expressed without reaction but silently in my ears "Please wait. you have to take a written examination".

I almost lost my optimism. While waiting to be called, I was observing many candidates. After interview, many were bid goodbye with the words that "you will hear from us soon". And here I am told to wait for a written test! Have I failed or passed?

After about 30 minute waiting I was sent to another room in the suite and was handed over a set of question papers to answer on. I found there were about four more in the room taking the exam.

I answered the question papers with my most sincerity. It was again quite a bit of Banking related, and few were of general intelligence and HR related. The time given was 30 minutes within which period I finished answering all questions.

Dr Menezes continued to be very courteous and bid me happy journey back without any reaction. He of course mentioned, candidates could be contacted by end September.

I came out of the hotel, removed my tie and jacket and went in front of Gateway of India, situated just in front of the hotel across the street. I was in no mood to roam the city of great attractions "Bombay" nor do any shopping. I took an auto to Bombay VT and went to ticket counter for a return ticket. I was not mentally prepared to sustain the painful journey of Lucknow to Bombay in unreserved compartment again. As I was in the queue waiting my turn, a broker came near me, probably seeing my decent clothing, and inquired if I need reservations. On knowing the destination is Lucknow, he volunteered to get me a reservation the same evening and will charge Rs 50. I consented instantly and bought a reserved berth. Had I stayed back a day more I would have spent few hundred rupees. So paying an extra Rs 50 appeared reasonable. I was back in Lucknow the day after morning, this time in a reserved compartment.

"The interview was real but the result is uncertain" was my answer to all inquisitive colleagues. I only confided in my wife that I did well in the interview and test.

Days passed. Months also passed. Information of possible contact by September by the bank was gone and it was almost end January of 1983. Lucknow witnessed a unprecedented cold winter. The house help we had from Odisha was gone. We had to leave our two and half-year-old daughter Payal in a crèche of not great standards without any option. Transfer back to Odisha was looking like a distant dream. Life was going thru quite a bit of complications and pessimism was sitting in.

On 24th January 1983 morning. Payal, our young daughter, was looking very weak and pale. She had

high fever. We obviously got concerned and did not wish to drop her in the crèche. Wife's responsibilities being higher, I volunteered to take off and be with the child. By evening there were marks in her face and body and it was a bout of measles. I stayed on leave for four days till she was partially cured. Hesitantly dropping her at the crèche in spite of her weakness, I went to office on the fifth day i.e. 28th January 1983. I was emotionally very disturbed both for the sickness of our daughter and the helplessness of budget living.

It was about 3 pm. Normally, most of the mails with important documents are received by an Officer in the bank for security and safety reasons so that it does not fall into wrong hands. Important mails those days, will come by registered mail where the recipient gives an acknowledgement. Post light launch, I was working on pending work of my four days absence when the Officer in charge of the mails department shouted in a high excited voice "Parija (as normally I was called) please come. There is some good news". At best I expected some pending reconciliation of bank accounts getting resolved. However, he handed me a thick bunch of papers. Though the registered mail was in my name, normally it is received by mail department. Without realizing it to be a personal mail, he opened it. And it was my appointment letter with Burgan Bank, Kuwait.

With excitement and inquisitiveness, I straight went to salary terms and I found it to be 15 times higher than my present Officer's salary which normally was considered high in those days. I definitely got butterflies in my stomach and there were instant congratulations from all employees in the branch. Suddenly I had become a hero having got a high paying job in an international bank abroad.

Mr Hanuman Singh, a very affable employee and a strong trade union leader suddenly reached the branch on a routine visit. He was extremely friendly to me and knowing the news, he immediately dialed my wife with exciting words that 'keep sweets ready, bhaiya has got a job abroad with 15 times more salary'. The news spread like wildfire.

By the time I reached the main branch to pick up my wife, people had already made many calculations like in one-month salary, I can buy a car and with four months' salary I can buy a house.

With the overall happiness of the proposed change in life, it sank in me of the next step. With both of us working and with the small child what exactly to plan. My wife volunteered that I should move forward and join the bank. She will continue with the job preferably in our home town of Odisha and will have our daughter with her.

The Regional Manager, who has to give a consent for inter-regional transfer, happily recommended and she promptly got her transfer orders to Bhubaneswar. I resigned the job and awaited formalities to complete and travel abroad.

xxxxxxxxxxxxxxxx

My mother's comment after she heard the news from me of my travelling abroad, was while both of us are in coveted jobs in one bank, why do I have to take the risk in a foreign land unknown and unexplored.

People in Odisha mostly knew London or America being foreign places. Anyone making it to either of the place are treated to be brilliant and successful. Middle East was not a very familiar place in Odisha unlike the entire western India and Northern India.

My wife told my mother that in Kuwait, alcohol is prohibited. That worked like magic. My mother, who was not happy with my frequent alcoholic misadventures was feeling very comfortable from this aspect. Hesitantly though, she happily agreed to my new foreign assignment.

There were many a hurdle. I never had a passport. It was nightmarish to get a passport in Lucknow. With constant support from an Oriya IAS Senior Bureaucrat friend, I could manage to get the passport after almost two months of getting the appointment letter. Visa processing in Kuwait had issues with my general profession of "service". I was needed to change the profession to "Accounts Professional". After that my passport had come with Emigration Clearance Required (ECR), a draconian and obsolete formality which was conveyed to me by Kuwait Embassy authorities. I had to run from pillar to post to make it change to Emigration Clearance Not Required (ECNR). Being refused for the removal of ECR from Passport Authorities of Lucknow and Bhubaneswar, I landed up at the Central Immigration office in Delhi. I was amazed by the approach of an official there who resolved my problem in a moment clearing it on the ground that I am a Post Graduate. The vast country of India still runs well with such type of proactive and helpful persons.

Finally, I landed in Kuwait on 13th August 1983 to a new chapter of my life.

Next seven years were memorable in Kuwait. Many ups and downs in the job, the happiness by end of the month when the salary gets credited to the account, excellent and inexpensive pure food, Financial comfort zone, social activity and helping people continued. Career growth was neither remarkable nor negative. It was a very normal growth trajectory contrary to my expectations which could be attributed partially to luck factor and circumstances.

The much expected house, car, foreign clothing and foreign gadgets were all part of life.

It was July 31st 1990 late evening. A close friend and colleague in the bank ASM Rao (fondly called Rao by me), had just returned from India leaving his new born son and wife in India to join him after few weeks.

He was the first friend of mine in Kuwait besides Jaganathan and we three bonded well for common thinking and intellectual chemistry matching.

We three along with Qadri, another batch mate used to travel together in my car every day to office. Getting a driving license those days was almost impossible. Passing the driving test in itself was a herculean task. I used to wake up at 5 am in the coldest of winter morning and go for the driving training. The Pakistani Punjabi Driving Trainer used to be very tough and ill behaved. May be it was intentional to make me learn safe driving to the best of my ability. I failed in my first attempt. Three attempts are allowed and if one fails getting a license door gets closed permanently. I got it in my second attempt fortunately with lot of compliments from the Police Officer taking my test for my immaculate driving. Driving license and car lifts you up few levels in society and is of extra convenience.

Kuwait was and still is a strictly alcohol prohibited country. While one can get a bottle from bootleggers at thirty times higher price, it was not worth the trouble. One can get a bottle of home brewed strong liquor made out of fermented grapes and apples. It used to be extra strong or few notches above the normal 41/42% alcohol in branded liquors. I invited ASM Rao to share the brew I had that evening. We drank the wine and spoke all about his experience back home in Hyderabad during his vacation.

There was mounting tensions between Kuwait and bordering country Iraq with strong diplomatic exchanges and strained relationship between the two countries. Iraq had just recovered from the aftermath of a decade old war with Iran and its serious economic negative impacts.

I got a call from our colleague Qadri from Delhi who was on vacation on that day about the reported rumor of strong boarder tensions between Kuwait and Iraq. It was almost 11 pm. I brushed him aside commenting that war was the least expected in civilized countries. Rao left for his apartment few blocks away by midnight. I slept off with the effect of home brewed wine.

At about 3.30 am I got up with severe sounds of firing as we were habituated seeing it in movies. I could easily understand that it was the sound of machine guns and other strong artillery products. I could conclude that probably Iraq has invaded Kuwait.

Jaganathan called me at about 4.30 am on land line which luckily both of us had, and inquired if what he thinks is the same as I think and it's an armed invasion by Iraq.

Our home at Abbasiya, a small growing up area in Kuwait was close to airport and hence the first point of attack by Iraq being the airport, obviously the gunfire was audible. The sounds of guns, tanks and missiles was deafening and spine chilling.

Few months back there was an uprising in Philippines and the then dictator Ferdinand Marcos was removed from power. Jaganathan used to remark during one of our hour long travel together to office every day, that we, in our lifetime have not witnessed an uprising or a people's revolution like Indian Independence Movement or the Russian uprising. Daringly we three, Jaganathan, Rao and myself started for office normally suited and booted. However, on approach to the city we found security men were not allowing any all vehicles inside the city and traffic was diverted back creating a massive traffic jam. Still uncertain of what is happening we drove thru the seafront and arrived at a senior colleague's villa where he was with his wife and two daughters. Mr Vijay Caleb, who was almost about 5 ranks senior to me in hierarchy in the bank had grown very friendly with me for my impressive work, humbleness and helping nature. I was with him when he had suffered a heart attack. From that day he would not go out anywhere other than office without me. I definitely enjoyed the love and affection of the entire family. Seeing three of us enter his villa, they did feel a sense of comfort during such uncertainties and phones were almost dead. Local television was off air. There were many low flying helicopters those were making ear shottering and scary sound. Kuwait being a tiny country with limited military force, could not resist the massive war machinery of Iraq.

By evening it was announced on BBC Radio, which was the only source to get news those days, that Kuwait has been illegally invaded by Iraq and occupied. Most of the rulers escaped to Saudi Arabia, unhurt.

Overnight all expatriate workforce become jobless and we all were uncertain of our future. The survival of next day was uncertain.

Myself and Rao moved over to Jaganathan's apartment as strongly suggested by him for feeling of safety and togetherness. Thanks to our daring nature, lesser tension being alone without family, we did manage to have sufficient food reserves and occasional bottles of alcohol that started flowing freely from Iraq.

Irrespective of the fear and tensions inside, we had a comfortable time, without jobs or office except few casual visits to office supposed to be under Iraqi personnel.

Forty-five days after the Iraqi occupation on August 1st 1990, non-communication with family and friends, we reached India traveling by car from Kuwait to Iraq, taking a flight to Amman, Jordan and being airlifted by Government of India from Jordan to Bombay.

Seven years of fabulous life and big earnings became zero overnight. We were refugees from Kuwait.

The arithmetic was very good with the reasonable savings, houses acquired in homeland with the seven years of rigorous savings and the confidence gained with the international exposure were all very valuable both arithmetically and mathematically.

● ● ●

THE BUSINESS INFINITY

It was extremely magnanimous of Bank Muscat, Sultanate of Oman, my immediate superior Mr. Ganeshan Sridhar and the real decision maker of the bank Mr. Ahmed Al Abry, the Chief Operating Officer, I was sent to study Advance Management Program (AMP) at World's best business school Harvard Business School, Boston, USA.

I was promoted to the post of the 4th Top Position of the Bank as Deputy General Manager, Corporate Banking Group competing with quite a few colleagues, mostly senior to me in age and as well as in years worked in the bank. It was the first time that the bank's Board of Directors appointed an external HR agency, based out of London to short list and select through a process of knowledge and leadership qualities for promotions to senior positions. I had already worked for 6 years as Asst General Manager with Bank Muscat post-merger of Bank Muscat with Commercial Bank of Oman where I worked. Irrespective of my initial hesitations and apprehensions, I was amazed to be treated exceptionally well by the top Management and Board of Directors of Bank Muscat post the merger. I was able to position myself well with the entire staff of juniors, peers and seniors in the new environment.

I went through the promotion process with total seriousness preparing myself fully well through studies and through mock interviews conducted by my colleagues so that I develop the confidence to face a high-octane interview board consisting of bank's Chairman, Deputy Chairman of the Board, CEO of the HR firm from London and the three top

Executives of the Bank; the CEO, Deputy CEO and COO. It was a rigorous one-hour interview where questions were fired from all directions and many a times unconnected to the flow. I have to admit that the top management of the Bank was quite positively getting inclined towards me and I could feel their generous way of navigation of the flow when questions were even remotely getting towards confrontation.

I always believed more questions in an interview allows better opportunity to express. Few minutes into the intense interview, I could get into the confidence of expressing myself better. I started enjoying the questions where in, I always got an opportunity to express better. Few times, I felt I extracted more and more questions from the highly senior and vastly experienced people. Interview was getting very positive and manly towards a inter active session.

One hour of scheduled interview got spilled into 40 minutes more as the Chairman of the selection committee, who also was the Chairman of Bank Muscat gave a rare comment that the interview appears very interactive and it should continue.

With warm thanks from each member of the Interview Panel, the interview ended with quite a positive feeling. Coming out and gulping two full glasses of water, I thanked God, thanked colleagues who barged into my room to enquire how did it go.

Results were expected in a week but very surprisingly by midday next day it flashed in the bank's internal mail that I have made it to the coveted post of heading the Corporate Banking Group that practically contributes about 80% of bank's business volume and revenue.

While my sincerity of being myself that obviously exuded honesty and genuineness, I felt inadequate in my knowledge levels for the coveted post that I was promoted to generously.

Work was my passion; philosophy and my prayer. My success of being a deal maker and provider of banking solutions in most adverse circumstances had made me quite acceptable to my peers, juniors and seniors.

The CEO of the bank Mr. Abdul Razak, the Deputy CEO Mr. Sunder George and the COO, Mr. Ahmed Al Abry, all of them developed a special acceptance for my never say die attitude, and extreme suave competence to do business.

Mr. Sunder George become a friend, philosopher and guide in life both professionally and personally.

Mr. Sridhar, my immediate boss, the General Manager, was meticulous, methodical and had sharp eyes for details.

He had a single advice to me that 1 should do business. Financing a brothel is fine if not on ethical grounds as long as it is feasible, viable and profitable. He will filter the credit process, legal process, risk management, Executive Management and the Board of Directors.

He had a deadly combination of aggressiveness without compromising the details. Mr. Sridhar will ask me a business plan and will patiently listen to my many alternatives. Instantly he will direct me to take the route that we both agree.

Mr. Sridhar perceived and directed me to work on a financial re-engineering plan of a reputed five-star Deluxe hotel which was on the verge of bankruptcy, not for the viability of the hotel but for unfortunate cyclic a business. We worked on a consolidation where in all liabilities for all banks were taken over by our bank. The cash flow of the hotel that can easily pay off the funding in ten years. In spite of reservation for the controlling bank in Oman and subsequent concerns by top management, I asked Mr. Sridhar whether we can still go ahead with the proposal of restructuring. His statement was with pure clarity that we will go ahead because we are convinced, we had done our due diligence with utmost sincerity and we are doing business with full fairness and without fear. This philosophy of him helped me in later part of my life when I was getting into issue based daring films.

Late afternoons used to be our interactions time that can be the happenings of the day, market conditions, near and midterm business plans or simple gossips. In one of my late evening interactions, I asked Mr. Sridhar if I can take two months sabbatical and go for further studies at my own cost. With higher responsibilities, I felt I must learn and equip myself better. He only inquired where I intend going and what is the cost estimate. My choice was to go Harvard Business School and obviously the cost was enormous.

Years before a close friend from Odisha, Kishore Dash, who was always a topper in studies had completed AMP at Harvard. He had joined in Kuwait in a moderate job without knowing his potential. In our first interaction in 1991, post liberation of Kuwait, I had opined that he is in the wrong place. Young and dynamic as he was, he took brave steps of career jumps and ended up in senior most financial position with one of the largest business group in Kuwait. Not satisfied there, he self-financed and did his stint at Harvard Business School. Educated and empowered, he later probably became the first Hindu to lead the largest Islamic Bank and Investment House in Middle East. I obviously was impressed with his enhanced knowledge levels and dreamed to join Harvard someday.

A paid leave would reduce my burden of the higher study expenses. Sridhar requested me to wait for a day. Next day by 11 am he called me to his cabin and congratulated me for some good news on the way. He advised me to see Mr. Ahmed Al Abry, the Chief Operating Officer.

The ever cool, composed person Mr. Al Abry was, and probably had stronger than the impenetrable Swiss Bank locker like mind. It is impossible to guess what he thinks. He warmly conveyed that the Bank will sponsor me with entire cost, full salary paid for the three months off from duty besides the perks I am eligible on a foreign tour. I got tears in my eyes for such benevolent gesture by the bank. Mr Al Abry had the Bank always his first priority in life, worked over 18 hours a day and always believed in people development who will become future leaders. I felt humbled that he considered me to be groomed to take higher responsibilities in future.

A highly qualified young executive of the bank and coincidentally from Odisha Mr. Manas Ranjan Das happily guided me through the rigorous admission process of Harvard Business School, Advance Management Program.

Thus, I landed at HBS with a cost to company of an amount probably I could have never afforded on my own.

The educational experience cannot be measured. I tried to take back as much as possible and, in the process, overstretched myself by studying 15 to 18 hours a day. Good counselling from the Professor to target to take back 30 to 40% of what I studied, relaxed me a bit and still I put an ambitious target of 40 to 50% take back. I tried to put on about 12 hours of studies a day including the six hours class room studies. I read to catch up on backlog on weekends instead of relaxing and freaking out like many others.

The three months passed like three weeks with hectic life of studies and quest to know more thru friendly interaction with many luminaries from various fields.

The day for me normally starts with waking up at 5.30 am and straight to gym by 6 am for an

Dean's Dinner Subject of "Change Makers" of Harvard Business School

hour of exercise. The walk of about 750 meters in the underground walking path or tunnel is a pleasure to commute. A futuristic structure connecting most buildings to each other thru an underground passage is reflective of the mind of the builders of the campus multiple decades back. The passage helps commuting during severe winter cold and when it is snowing.

Back to room by 7 am followed by a quick shower and the best of breakfast at the dining hall. The spreads used to be elaborate with items from most parts of the world. We are ready for the class at 8 am, most of us carrying a large glass of best brewed black coffee. Classes, though very intense, but gets over without realizing the time due to high interactive case study method.

Over next two months it was learning bliss. Every moment, every interaction, every class, every function was like digging gold mine of knowledge. The last four days into the class was interactive learning as to who I am and where I wish to go.

And I did. I become a change maker Alumni of HBS doing something significant so be the example in Deans List and Alumni Cover. Both arithmetic and Mathematics were and are the greatest of my life time.

● ● ●

Stories

03 MAR 2014

A LIFE TRANSFORMED

Akshay Kumar Parija has come far from his boyhood village in India. A successful businessman, he's now producing movies with social themes that help preserve his native Odisha culture.

Re: Akshay Parija (AMP 172); By: Robert S. Benchley

Topics: Entrepreneurship-Corporate Entrepreneurship
Finance-Banks and Banking
Information-Biography
Organizations-Corporate   Social Responsibility and Impact
Philanthropy-Giving Impact   Leadership-General
Entertainment-Film Society-Culture Operations-Distribution
Personal Development-General

It's a long way—a very long way—from the village of Balidhip, in the eastern Indian state of Odisha, to Cambridge, Massachusetts. When you grow up without roads, electricity, or running water, when light and darkness control the rhythms of your life, and when you are so cut off from the outside world that you have only the spark of your intellect to tell you that there must be something more, the distance seems even greater.

Akshay Kumar Parija (AMP 172, 2007) describes growing up in Balidhip in the late 1950s and early 1960s: "We rose and slept with the sun," he says. "Lying in bed at night, all we heard were the sounds of insects and the flutes played by the night watchmen who cared for cows and buffalo. We were afraid of the dark, because we heard stories about witches and goblins eating people caught outside after sundown.

"My father did almost nothing to earn money, so we were dependent on a meager income from the land. Our school was a seven-kilometer walk in each direction. With little food, it was difficult to have the energy to walk that distance every day. During the monsoon floods, we wore a towel-like garment called a gamuchha and carried our school clothes above our heads to keep them dry. Wading through the water, we had to watch out for snakes that had been driven from their homes by the flooding."

Civilization was only 60 kilometers away, in the state capital of Cuttack, where Parija's uncle lived.

"I took the eight-hour bus ride to visit him twice when I was a boy," he recounts. "At home, we ate rice and could only afford roti, a type of bread, on holidays. I thought my uncle must be rich, because his family ate roti every night.

"I saw billboards for the first time and bragged to my friends back in Balidhip that the products they advertised were the names of movies I had seen. An older boy knew that one of them was the name of a ringworm ointment, so I was caught in my lie, and they all laughed at me. That revelation of my ignorance was the most humiliating moment of my childhood."

Still, Parija says, life in his remote village endowed him with four qualities—hope, optimism, determination, and self-motivation—that have carried him far from his roots. After leaving home, earning two degrees at universities in India, and working as an international banker for nearly three decades, Parija finally closed the distance and found his way to HBS.

His journey began with books. "We had no newspaper or TV," he says, "so I started reading books that would give me an idea of the world outside. I knew I could not change my destiny to be born there, but I also knew that with hard work I could change my future. I studied hard, came out on top in my final exams, received a scholarship, and left for college."

Parija attended BJB College, a state school with low fees, where he majored in economics and political science, graduating in 1974. He took a clerical job at a local Indian bank and enrolled in a master's program in public administration at Utkal University, receiving his degree in 1978. During that time, he also took courses in banking and finance, which enabled him to be promoted to a managerial position.

With little room for career growth at the bank where he worked, Parija began looking outside India and won a position with a bank in Kuwait against nearly 2,000 other applicants. It was there that Parija came to the attention of two high-level executives who were HBS alumni—Aubyn Hill (MBA 1978) and Amal Wahab (MBA 1987).

"I was extremely impressed with these two men, their knowledge level, style of management, clarity of thought, and leadership abilities," says Parija. "In fact, it was then that I set my sights on someday attending HBS."

Hill subsequently became CEO of a bank in Oman and took Parija with him.

"In seven years, we did wonders by converting a bankrupt institution into the number-one bank in the country," says Parija, who later became head of corporate banking following a merger that created a much larger institution. "My contribution to the bank's income was significant, and I was rewarded with company-paid business education," he says. "I chose the AMP program. My dream had come true."

Although Parija had already acquired decades of business acumen, HBS was a transformational experience for him.

"It taught me how to set a goal and work toward it, and it gave me the courage to become an entrepreneur," he says. "A group of us founded Blue Lines Shipping Group in 2010. We owned eight tankers, and transported petroleum products and dry bulk commodities all over the world. In 2010, Lloyd's gave us an award as best ship operator in the Middle East and on the Indian subcontinent.

"I am proud to say that HBS had a tremendous influence on who I am today," Parija says. "I wish I could say I brought back 60 or 70 percent of what I studied, but there was so much. In all honesty, I probably brought back only 40 percent, but it was enough, and it made me very rich."

One final payoff from AMP for Parija: it put him in touch with his creative side. Now he is using his wealth to finance films, mostly with social and environmental themes, that preserve his native Odisha culture. Working with acclaimed Indian writer-director Prashant Nanda, he has produced two films to date. For his first, The Living Ghost (2010), Parija received a Silver Lotus award from Pratibha Patil, then president of India. He is currently working on a serial and has two more projects in the pipeline.

"I believe it is a corporate social responsibility to pay back to your motherland," Parija says. "I am fortunate that I have the resources to bring a rich cultural heritage to the world forum.

"Through my films, I hope to create an awareness in the world about the threat of climate change, the need for environmental protection, the legacy we leave for future generations, and the importance of having respect for all human beings."

Today, living in Dubai, far from Balidhip in measures more significant than distance, Parija reflects on how the lessons he learned at HBS strengthened the experiences of his childhood.

"I saw the wretched condition in which so many people live," he says, "and how they struggle to have a good meal or a good education. It motivated me to try to see that no village remains dark, that no small boy loses out in life because he has no access to proper study material, that no family is too poor to eat roti.

"My life as a boy was simple—primitive, by most standards—but it taught me to appreciate nature, it taught me how to be alone yet feel happy, and it taught me how to identify my priorities in life and always aim higher."

● ● ●

THE JOURNEY TO DESTRUCTION

It was a cold winter midnight at Bhubaneswar during December 2013. With few close friends of over fifty plus years of friendship I had a very warm, interactive and nostalgic evening in suite 314 of Hotel Crown. The best of exclusive alcohol was not in shortage being well stocked in the room, thanks to the privilege allowed by the Hotel Owner Mr Rohit Das. The specially hand cooked snacks and food by the celebrity Chef Mr Rahim was flowing whenever desired. We were six of us from my young banking days at Cuttack. When I first landed at Cuttack, being transferred from my earlier posting at Bissam Cuttack in Indian Overseas Bank (IOB), I obviously did not know any one at Cuttack other than my family and relatives.

In Cuttack branch of IOB, I quickly became popular probably due to my young age and youthfulness besides for my wons efficiency. During the phase of a couple of years in Cuttack, I became close to many young friends who created their own moderate identity in work or business. I connected well with quite few of people both emotionally and intellectually. We remain bonded for over five decades and during most of my visits to Bhubaneswar, one evening was always reserved for a get together in the hotel.

It was one of those evenings of great friendship time with a bit of extra drinking and eating. The party got extended to midnight. As is said 'among old friends talks or topics' never end.

Back to the lobby to bid farewell to friends past midnight, I was told by the reception staff that a couple came to meet me and since I was busy with friends, they preferred not to interfere but to wait. They were hesitant to sit in the lobby and opted to wait outside the gate. Anxious, I walked down the path to the gate in the cold night and found a couple of husband and wife waiting. I could immediately recognize the man being the Make Up Artist of Thukul. He visited Muscat with the entire team for the Thukul shoot. I was very disturbed knowing that he had a bad medical condition with unfortunate Cancer and his mouth after operations was half stitched. He cannot eat solid food. The day they were at home, I made a healthy smoothie of various fruits with milk and sugar. He had tears in his eyes while drinking it. He always narrated it to people back home making me a hero which I am not worth.

I forced them to come in and inquired about their visit. He hesitantly shared that he requires regular source of income to manage his costly treatment and family welfare. While the talk went on with various matters but I had heard nothing. My mind was in a spin and blocked. I was thinking about him and thru him was thinking about many others who could be in similar state of affairs. Films were few and could give hardly a month of employment. Then they are jobless and almost starving.

My alcoholic high spirit was gone. He was the person whose hard work got me National Award and State Awards. He was awarded the Best Make Up Award in the State Film Award. And now he is struggling in life after making hero of me and many more in the past.

I promised him to do whatever I can do and came back to room devastated. Is this the fate of Odisha's Cine World? People were made stars, superstars and rich by climbing the pyramid of the lower down supporting people like make-up men, light-men, sounds-men and many others. But today we don't know how many are suffering in silence with multiple agonies of poverty or and sickness!!

I could not sleep. I was extremely disturbed. My principles and my Harvard education taught me a 360-degree welfare of society. And here there were so many suffering silently.

Though I fell asleep in early hours of morning, I woke at about 7 PM and after refreshing, went to Mr Prasant Nand's house. Since I had not called him about my coming, he was a bit surprised. I narrated him the entire experience of the earlier evening. He was calm. He asked me straight what really is troubling me. There are so many people in distress. How many people I can support!!

To my inquiry of how I can be of general support so that the unfortunate phenomenon can be limited if not completely eliminated.

He was thoughtful for some time as he also was very much agonized with many such incidences.

He made a suggestion that I should probably try to be in Television space. It will obviously create lot of employment. People will remain employed for long term with regular income. Indirectly at least few of likely occurring cases like the make-up artist will get neutralized.

It appeared to be as a wonderful suggestion. We agreed that he will touch base with few experienced directors and EPs (Executive Producers) in General Entertainment Channels.

Tarang of Odisha Television Group was the highest TRP leading Channel. The earlier prominent ETv Odiya was on back foot due to few competition issues. Another privately owned Channel was Sarthak TV which was showing promise of coming up.

Since I did not know anyone in any of the Channels personally, Durga Acharya who was Assistant Director in the film Jianta Bhoota and Thukul under Mr Prasant Nanda approached me hearing our interest for Television Serials. He was working as EP with Tarang and was expecting few new Serials being planned by Tarang Management.

The plan for getting commissioned for a serial at Tarang progressed very positively and within two weeks after few of the meetings with top executives of the channel, I signed my first Serial 'Sahanai' to be produced for Tarang.

Though it appeared to be similar to making films involving shoots, editing, BGM etc the business model and mathematics was completely different.

In Hindi Television production scenario, the Producer pitches for a story to the Channel and if the subject of Story is attractive, the Channel commissions the Producer for making the Serial by selecting the entire Cast and Crew. In Regional space like Odisha, the Channel provides the story, selects most of the Characters and even strongly refers some senior crews. Though they also identify the Director, for my first Serial, it was already decided to rope in Mr Prasant Nanda to direct. It was obviously a big break for the Channel to be able to bring in the Legend of Celluloid to small screen.

Mr Nanda plunged into the making of TV serial. It was learning for him as well as me. He put all his creative expertise to visualize the story path and went on shooting significant amount of stocks irrespective of the story line provided. His vision was to make it as good as his films.

Months later and significant amount already being spend on outdoors, I met the Channel people. By that time, I had already built one of the biggest Studio Floors at Kateni, Kantabada just 19 km away from heart of Bhubaneswar, in the land of Sri Rohit Das. The land was adjacent to his big farm but was a bit disputed. He agreed to sell it to me once all records set right but till such time he signed a long term lease agreement to be converted to sell in due course. Badly cheated by the construction contractor who clearly cheated me due to my ignorance and unfortunately died in a road accident, the Studio got built as a massive structure, one of its kind in Odisha. Shooting shifted into indoors but unfortunately the Channel Executives found the products that came out was not in compatibility to their Serial Storyline. In one go 35 Episodes which ideally would have been billed for at least Rs 50 lacs was thrown away.

It became an enhanced determination that we must be on air with the serial. With all the changes, new story, new shoots we streamed the serial 'Sahanai' on 14th April 2014.

The Serial 'Sahanai' became a super success and rose to be the Number One TRP rated Serial among the 7 Serials run by the Channel.

During the time another Serial named 'To Aganara Tulasi Mu" with Sarthak was ruling being the highest TRP leader continuously.

When I was congratulated being number one in Tarang Channel, I had humbly commented that my vision and ambition is to be number one in whole Odisha among all GEC Channels.

I did it with my next Serial ' Nua Bohu' thanks to the efforts of Mr Satyajit Mohapatra who was Fiction Head. He unfortunately died during Covid 19.

I did a serial for Colors ' Aaina' with a disastrous financial loss due to terrible mismanagement by the staff looking after the production.

I built two more massive Studio Sets and today it's the biggest Studio Complex in Odisha after the Government owned Kalinga Studio.

Unfortunate and avoidable, I got into a financial dispute with Tarang. I felt in the excitement of showing money making or money saving, the then CFO, harassed me with some illegal deductions. I was so emotionally hurt with the treatment that I offered to walk out of the project. Unfortunately, the rich owners never saw reasoning and I closed my relationship with Tarang Channel. Much later the same Executive was arrested by Police for financial wrong doing and was in jail though for few days. Loyalty to your organization is good but hurting others below belt for benefit of organization and your own glory are sins.

There is always a poetic justice, and god penalized him years later.

As I was having no work and the massive studios were idle, came the angels in disguise. Sarthak private channel was bought over by Zee Group and a new professional team was on the ground. They created TRP history with their value addition in product quality enhancement.

I already had the reputation of losing money but ensuring the best quality production. Many crores of losses had already happened by that time. Thanks to my work and business abroad, I was able to still continue losing money but make quality products.

Zee Sarthak, as the Channel was named by that time post acquisition by Zee of Sarthak, approached me to work for them. It was a much desired blessing in disguise.

The ambitious serial they were planning to launch could be shot only in one of my studio floors. It was built as a massive structure to shoot high class reality shows. Unfortunately, the floor which was leased to Colors Channel was prematurely canceled for the Channel's internal management problems without any consideration to the big capital investment I had done. The serial for Colors executed by us was a financial disaster of crores of rupees purely due to the callous behavior of their Channel Head and his unfortunate irresponsible handling by Channel People as well as well as my supervisors.

Zee Sarthak was very cautious with the investments to be made to construct the set inside and they planned that the show must run for two years to recover the money.

New set of Executives in Dwipayan Majumdaar and Ahna Chakravoty joined the Channel Zee Sarthak and practically handheld us to launch the Serial. It became a great hit and topped the TRP chart.

More than the financial gain, I earned the respect from the Channel for our commitment to good quality work. A year down we were allotted one more Serial by the Channel which though did not top the TRP list but earned great popularity. The Serial won 6 Awards in the State Tele Award competition.

After two more Serials the Channel perceived the Biggest Tele Serial Show in Odisha.

Such show was never done before and was perceived to be the greatest show ever.

The Programming Head Mr Srijit Satpathy, a very youthful, dashing, dynamic, creative and genuine in heart and a great visionary started discussing with me on the dream project.

"Only in your set it can be done and only Producer is you in Odisha who can do it" was his answer to my question why did he choose me.

Both Srijit and me had excellent chemistry and on many an occasions we would find that our thinking and planning was same.

Srijit wished the serial to have the 4 decade reigning superstar of Odisha Sri Sidhant Mohapatra to be the Protagonist. Sidhant to come to small screen!! Almost wishful thinking. Why a superstar like him will opt to come to television space????

Srijit narrated the story to Mr Sidhant Mohapatra. Apparently he was fascinated with the story. But why should he compromise?

With authority and support from the dynamic Channel Head Mr Arghya Ray Chowdhury, I called on Mr Sidhant Mohaptra on a week end early morning. Being a terrific disciplinarian he was happy to see me early morning. Hs wife, in herself a big star, served me an excellent breakfast.

After it I made him an offer which he could not refuse!!!

Kemiti Kahibi Kaha (KKK) took birth creating history in Odisha. The trailer and teaser was with Helicopter and Powerboats, unseen in Odisha. The lady protagonist was the popular face Supriya. The well-known and accomplished film Director Susant Mani took the mantle of direction.

Kemiti Kahibi Kaha became a phenomenon for the Odiya audience not only in Odisha but Pan India. But every month I was in unfortunate negative cash flows.

Covid 19 created havoc. However, KKK continued with popularity.

A serial of that dimension with the superstar and other big stars became obviously a bone in throat for competitors. Everything was done to derail the project.

Project got completed with almost one and half year run. It was not the highest TRP ranker but remained within the top three.

However, making such a big show was making a big hole in my pocket. But as a professional commitment I took all the losses to complete the show of about five hundred plus episodes.

It was during Mid-June, 2021, I was approached by India's biggest entertainment channel Star Plus. They were intending to enter Odiya viewer space and were planning to launch an Odiya GEC Channel.

Excellent in creativity and ambition, they aimed to take Odiya entertainment to a new level of popularity.

Where ever Star Group went in India, they grew to be number one rated channel.

They expressed to bring in new concepts of fiction and non-fiction shows which have been not made by existing channels in Odisha.

Coincidentally Mr Srijit Satpathy joined Star Plus as Program Head.

Knowing his creativity and dynamism, it was appearing a significant association to create wonders.

Our production house had over 7000 episodes' experience. We had our own studios and facilities, zero off air record and overall high Ratings for all our Serials in the past.

Obviously we were the first choice to work for Star Plus to produce the Fiction Shows.

During our interaction with the local Programming Team, it was highly motivating to be associated with the most popular channel. At the same time, we assumed that Star Plus will not be tight fisted but will spend liberally.

As a result, we deployed significant amounts to build and renovate our sets and installed central air conditioning which was a requirement for the Channel.

They also had quite a few stipulations of international standard besides the process of shooting including staff welfares.

Odisha teleworld was not habituated to the luxury of Mumbai or Kolkota. The amount just paid to the writer per episode is the total cost of a Tele Episode in Odisha.

The price almost continued for last two decades. While all cost would have doubled or tripled, the episodic payment by channels would have hardly gone up by about 10 to 25%.

Producers obviously made good profit in early days when artist cost or shooting cost used to be much lower. Many have retired in the absence of good profit. Many opt to work at cost or marginal losses as they have built big infrastructures.

Persons like us made entry at a time when making cost had skyrocketed without corresponding increase in episodic cost.

As such, I made massive losses in the beginning and continued taking new work hoping to recover but always ended up with higher losses.

Being not conversant of market rates, not able to personally supervise the execution not able to get the right and experienced staff, few unscrupulous people took advantage and looted money till they were caught.

Starplus meetings were highly inspiring listening out their business plan, vision and promises for Odisha to bring in a renaissance of entertainment. Passionate as I am always for growth, visibility for quality products, I had no hesitation in instantly agreeing to work with Starplus.

Though not explicitly, I got a feeling that the Channel would like to use our production house as well as our massive Studio set exclusively. The big investment done on three floors in a composite Studio complex was always a challenge to get full deployment.

With excellent communications and creative chemistry with Srijit, expression of total confidence on our capacity by the top level executives of Star, especially due to our track record of performance over a decade with zero default, I got optimistic of of an opportunity of life to make a strong positioning in regional Television space like Ekta Kapoor, the idol of any aspiring Production House.

I forgot the word 'no' and agreed to the massive quantitative and qualitative requirements by the local top executives of Programming.

Crores were spent for renovations and central air conditioning of the Sets, which was not prevalent in

Odisha earlier. A highly humid place, the look of perfection of an artist was getting disturbed with sweating. I was very pleased with the technical excellence of Star and instantly agreed to convert all my Sets with central air-conditioning.

Earlier the relaxing room, make up room and costume room used to be air-conditioned. Floor area used to be normal.

Out of the four new fictions of daily soap opera, proposed by Starplus, we were allotted two thus almost doing 50% of the work of the Channel.

Our visibility got a momentum and the production house suddenly become known pan India. We got silent feeler of partnership for Mumbai and South.

Then came the first shock. The commercial team handling finance from Kolkata, approved a ridiculous budget that collapsed our ambition and optimism.

It was like Programming Team asking for nothing less than diamond and Commercial Team approving a peanuts budget.

Market went hot. Artists who are normally paid a specific market driven price started demanding four times, and some or many of them who had right strings were obliged by the channel.

A very poorly planned Channel Opening, without proper content backing, Kolkata executives who had no knowledge of Odisha, started buying extremely poor and stray films which were otherwise rejected by existing channels in Odisha. Brokers in between reported to have made millions.

Markets of Odisha and even Kolkata went berserk with perception that money is flying in Odisha from Starplus for any trash product.

Some if not all, made a beautiful day with their below average films with hefty money.

Money was everywhere flying other than to us who were genuine and quality film makers and have invested into be the long term partners. Channels don't grow with films but with their fiction shows. While presumably money flew, people like me were sadly deprived of our legitimate dues.

We went on deploying excess money over the budget with hope to win the confidence of Programming People for long term association.

Unfortunately, Commercial in Kolkata had different mindset and they were insensitive of our agony and losses.

Starplus decided to fold up in six months, a humiliating experience for them in India.

Heads rolled. Top executives blamed for the scam of buying undeserving contents were all suspended or terminated.

A dream of working next ten years was shattered overnight. All shows were suspended.

We were left with a loss of over Rs 7.6 crores. Too little in Mumbai or India standards. But it was the dal roti of few moderate but ambitious producers like us whose backbone was broken.

First time in history of over a decade, we defaulted in our payments and still there are dues to pay.

Over the brief association with Star Plus, we invested about Rs 13 crores, got hardly Rs 5.4 crores thus loosing Rs 7.6 crores.

Our appeals, court cases were sadly and badly denied with their massive power.

All our appeals and mails remained unreplied.

Starplus paid us for the episodes we made.

But what about the massive scrapping of episodes for no fault of ours where we were bulldozed to accept losses???

What about the high investments done to studios with promise of a ten-year association?

We continue to cry till date while Star Plus got into a new bed!!!!

Neither Arithmetic nor Mathematics were right. It was a disaster.

Neither Arithmetic nor Mathematics were right. It was a disaster.

● ● ●

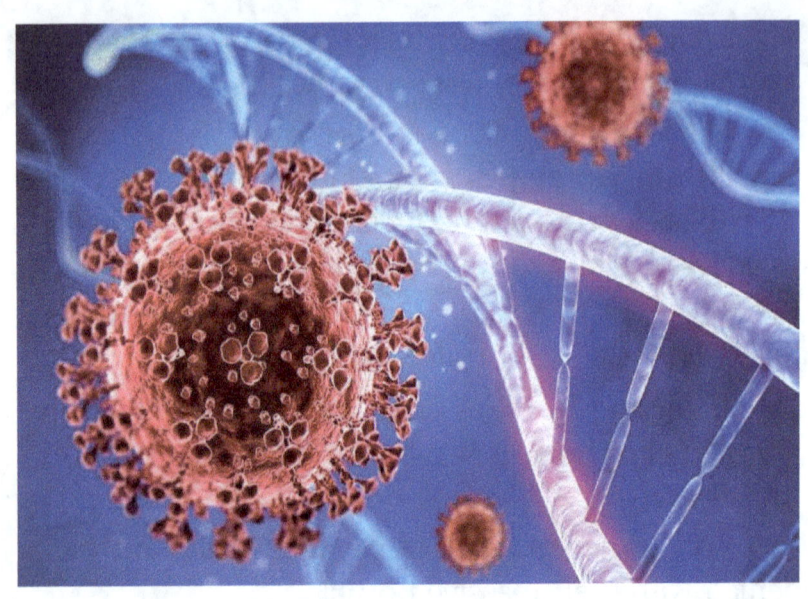

AMID THE CATASTROPHE

Being a Wednesday, my cook and caretaker at home allows me to eat non-veg breakfast.

The home that I mean is my free stay in a luxurious apartment at Unit-8, Bhubaneswar popularly known as Pinnacle Apartment.

Three decades back, the only landmark in Unit-8, Bhubaneswar, the State Capital, was DAV school, Unit -8 and the first Kalyan Mandap in Odisha conceived and built by the then most popular and most controversial politician Sri Basant Biswal. Mr. Biswal with development and service to people as main agenda, probably replicated the Kalyan Mandap concept, quite prevalent in South India for holding every type of functions at a low price. It is a matter of satisfaction to observe that hundreds of Kalyan Mandaps have mushroomed in Bhubaneswar today be it legally or illegally.

Pinnacle Apartment is situated next to the old and well known Kalyan Mandap in front of DAV School, Unit-8.

Ten years back when the building was launched and emerging as a landmark apartment building being located at such a strategic place, I too had inquired with the builder who politely told me that the price is too high and I may not be able to afford it. Of course, when I mentioned that I live in Middle East and already have two apartments in that area he immediately became receptive and provided all information. I got fascinated to buy one but somehow was diverted into too much other activities to focus on the investment.

Thru a long process of bonding over decades I was already like a family member of Late Sri Rohit Kumar Das, owner of Hotel Crown in Bhubaneswar.

Due to our strong closeness, he insisted to me in 2002 that whenever I visit Odisha, I must stay in his hotel for multiple reasons like safety, medical emergency, ease of living besides great food of my choice.

I lived in Hotel Crown for 17 years from 2002 till 2019 and the hotel became my home and address in Bhubaneswar.

My daughter's marriage, my mother's 11th day rituals after her demise and my celluloid journey's first function, all of them were held in this hotel.

Well-wishers and fans will write letters with my name and the hotel address.

Aspirants for Cinema or Serial world would carefully cultivate staff in hotel to known if I am in town.

It was coincidental that I visualized extended stays in Odisha by mid-2019 due to proposed expansion in my film and serial activities.

I aimed to take up an apartment to use partly as office and partly as guest house so as to reduce my extra eating and drinking in Crown, famous for its extraordinary food.

The building that came to my immediate radar was the Pinnacle Building which was almost completed by 2019. I also came to know that the apartments are fairly large compared to standard 1200 to 1800 Sq Feet apartment sizes in Bhubaneswar.

On enquiry I was happy to know that the land owner of the building was the family of Late Sri Basant Biswal.

Over past fifteen years, there was a close bonding that had developed with the family members of Late

Sri Biswal, partially due to the close matrimonial family relationship and partly due to my personal faith and encouragement for the political activity of both the sons of late Sri Biswal.

I called on the younger brother Sri Ranjib Biswal, who was married to a close relative, was a celebrity cricketer, cricket administrator and political leader being the youngest elected Member of Parliament at one time. I wished to explore the possibilities of buying an apartment in the building.

Savvy and energetic as he is always, he strongly suggested me not to deploy crores plus to buy an apartment, but better lease an apartment belonging to the family. The lease price he indicated is significantly economical.

I approached his elder brother Sri Chiranjib Biswal, the sitting MLA and working President of Congress with whom I had also developed good communications, again through family relationships and common intellectual thinking.

Chiranjib babu was extremely enthusiastic to agree to lease me the apartment. I was thrilled to know that the building has very few apartments with large area of about 3000 sq ft. and one of them is the one he is offering me. The place somewhat resembled the typical luxury apartments in Dubai besides being very much Vastu compliant. He directed me in his typical affable way to plan the move to stay and will tell me the rent later, once I am settled.

After my proper relocation to the apartment, Pinnacle, Mr. Chiranjib Biswal threw an emotional Bomb refusing to take any rent.

As a seasoned Politician he discarded all my pleadings and used all friendly emotional reasons that I should shift into the place and enjoy staying.

Had I not been moved, it could have been disastrous during Covid 19 lockdown that struck the World hardly after 5 months of my shifting. Hotels were closed in the world. I know I would have happily continued in Hotel Crown but would have been the only guest in the entire hotel complex.

I started my preparations to move to the apartment by 4th quarter of 2019 much to the strong objection and sadness of Sri Rohit Das. As I was staying in hotel for about 18 years I had to buy minimum furnishing and requirements to be settling in, into a new living place.

xxxxxxxx

The move-in in was smooth, seamless and I enjoyed the new place immensely.

Six months' down came Covid-19. I was to travel back to Dubai on 19th March but the lockdown started from 20th, march and I was stuck in Bhubaneswar.

I had an extremely relaxed time in the apartment with my Cook, Housekeeper and a closely acquainted lady Ritika, who carefully shuttled between her house and my new location and ensured my convenience and well-being. Unfortunately, there were few issues that care up between us that created a strong emotional misunderstanding which remains unresolved till date.

Covid/ Corona came and still life went on with full speed. 5/E Pinnacle became identified with me. Mr. Biswal continued to refuse rent and always evaded the topic in his persuasive manner.

Neither purchased nor paying rent, still I became visible owner of a Multicore apartment.

By 2021, the new house boy and cook, Karunakara joined me as the relocation to India was declined by my old houseboy of Muscat and Dubai for over 15 years.

From day one Karunakar turned out to be a meticulously organised person, too religious and highly caring.

His Prayer rituals and worshipping starts at 5 am. And by the time I wake up, the apartment gives an extremely aesthetic, pious, and peaceful feeling.

Almost two rooms are converted to temples and all religious festivals are strictly followed in the house as insisted by him.

Only Wednesday, Fridays and Sundays non-veg food allowed to be cooked at home.

Karunakar, by his extreme hard work and following strong religious rituals also infused a sense of discipline in me.

So on 22nd Septmber being a Wednesday I had the luxury to have my favourite puffy egg omelette and roasted millet bread, which he collects from Adisha, the Government Outlet for ethnic food. Bread and Omelette is always a luxury breakfast for me.

As I go to office at 9 am, it was usual routine of prayers in front of very small Mandir set up at the entrance of the office and then bowing before the images of Lord Jagannath, Sirdi Sai Baba and an illuminated Mata Vaishnodevi I start the work.

The day was extremely busy. My new founded premium OTT platform was conceived, perceived, and about to take birth on 15th October 2022.

It was mentally and emotionally stressful working on various contents in a short period of time as the platform needed boost by way of new contents. The entire team of KancchaLannka was operating out of my office.

Normally I go for a simple lunch to home by about 1.30 pm and resume work upto about 9 pm.

On this day I was extremely tied up with my disastrous assignment of two mega Serials by StarPlus's new Odiya Channel Star Kiron. I was almost already at a loss of over Rs 6.00 Crores over and above the pressure of the quality work to be made to meet telecast deadlines. The Kolkata office which controls the finance would not pay and the local office due to their quality and rating compulsions would demand the best of products where in the cost gets badly escalated.

It was like sitting on a tiger where in, one cannot get down, lest, the tiger will eat or continue suffering uncontrolled losses.

Our Chief Operating Officer and myself were embroiled in multiple dilemmas of execution and organizing funding in the face of badly depleted personal savings. I had already sold some properties and vehicles to fund the losses.

At 2 PM, before my delayed travel home for lunch, I got a what's up message. It was from an acquaintance in Facebook accepted as friend almost two years back during boring Corona Lockdown days, with whom I did not have any communications in the recent past. Her very casual wishes occasionally remain non replied by me.

I somehow read the message and was taken aback.

The What's Up message changed the course of my life, my finances, and my reputation.

Over the course of next one month it was worse than a lightening strike, thunder, rain and cyclonic storm on my emotional life.

Major part of the problems got resolved, but my reputation took a heavy beating, that would require years to heal.

There were decisions to be taken which would create havoc of my reputations. I took the decision on three mathematical calculations:

First: People who were, are and will remain genuine friends, will remain same irrespective of my reputation or during challenging times.

Second: People whose opinion and impression swings, were never my friends and its absolutely immaterial for me whether they continue to be friends or not.

Third: Truth will always be the winner.

Probably in whole of India, it still remains the first ever case with remarkable justice in my favor.

However, arithmetic, mathematics, or personal prudence, everything went wrong for a short while and finally truth prevailed.

● ● ●

Akshay K Parija was always perceived to be kind, humble, stylish, glamorous, fun loving, man with all costly hubbies; be it clothes, shoes, watches, cars or women!!!!!

Friends appreciate him for his openness!!

There also friends who describe him as misogynist, womanizer, debauch, arrogant and rude!!

The script will be unfold in the next book!!!

As we release this book to readers , our film has entered the 98th Oscar Race as well as Golden Globe Race 2026

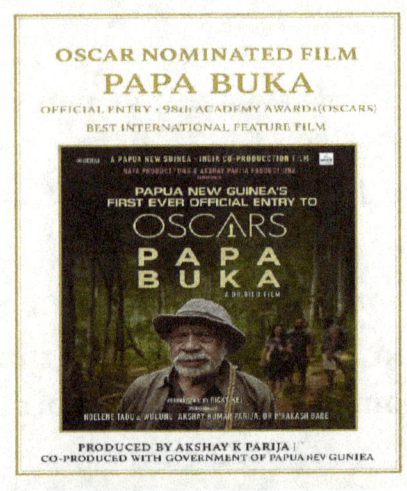

www.ingramcontent.com/pod-product-compliance
Lightning Source LLC
Chambersburg PA
CBHW052139070526
44585CB00017B/1890